PROBLEMS OF RUNAWAY YOUTH

Publication Number 985
AMERICAN LECTURE SERIES®

A Publication in
The BANNERSTONE DIVISION *of*
AMERICAN LECTURES IN SOCIAL AND REHABILITATION PSYCHOLOGY

Editors of the Series

RICHARD E. HARDY, Ed.D.
Diplomate in Counseling Psychology (ABPP)
Chairman, Department of Rehabilitation Counseling
Virginia Commonwealth University
Richmond, Virginia

and

JOHN G. CULL, Ph.D.
Director, Regional Counselor Training Program
Department of Rehabilitation Counseling
Virginia Commonwealth University
Fishersville, Virginia

The American Lecture Series in Social and Rehabilitation Psychology offers books which are concerned with man's role in his milieu. Emphasis is placed on how this role can be made more effective in a time of social conflict and a deteriorating physical environment. The books are oriented toward descriptions of what future roles should be and are not concerned exclusively with the delineation and definition of contemporary behavior. Contributors are concerned to a considerable extent with prediction through the use of a functional view of man as opposed to a descriptive, anatomical point of view.

Books in this series are written mainly for the professional practitioner; however, academicians will find them of considerable value in both undergraduate and graduate courses in the helping services.

PROBLEMS OF RUNAWAY YOUTH

JOHN G. CULL

RICHARD E. HARDY

CHARLES C THOMAS • PUBLISHER
Springfield • Illinois • U.S.A.

Published and Distributed Throughout the World by
CHARLES C THOMAS • PUBLISHER
Bannerstone House
301-327 East Lawrence Avenue, Springfield, Illinois, U.S.A.

© *1976 by* CHARLES C THOMAS • PUBLISHER
ISBN 0-398-03425-7
Library of Congress Catalog Card Number: 75-4920

Library of Congress Cataloging in Publication Data
Main entry under title:
Problems of runaway youth.

(American lecture series; publication no. 985)
Includes bibliographies and index.
1. Runaway youth—United States. 2. Juvenile delinquency—United
States. 3. Social work with youth—United States. I. Cull, John G. II.
Hardy, Richard E.
[DNLM: 1. Runaway reaction. WS462 P964]
HQ196.P75   362.7'3   75-4920
ISBN 0-398-03425-7

Printed in the United States of America
M-3

This book is dedicated to wonderful friends

Campbell and Anne Hardy

of

Jacksonville, Florida

and

Dr. and Mrs. Davis Y. Paschall

of

Williamsburg, Virginia

CONTRIBUTORS

DAVID L. AIKEN
Correspondent for *The Advocate*

GERALD R. BISSIRRI
Chief Psychologist
Division of Adolescent Medicine
Childrens Hospital of Los Angeles
Los Angeles, California

WILLIAM M. BREER
Probation Officer
San Bernardino County, California

JOHN G. CULL, Ph.D.
Director
Regional Counselor Training Program
Department of Rehabilitation Counseling
Virginia Commonwealth University
Fishersville, Virginia

JAMES O. FINCKENAUER, Ph.D.
Professor of Criminal Justice
Chairman
Department of Criminal Justice
Trenton State College
Trenton, New Jersey

DALE C. GARELL, M.D.
Director
Division of Adolescent Medicine
Childrens Hospital of Los Angeles
Los Angeles, California

RICHARD E. HARDY, Ed.D.
Diplomate in Counseling
Psychology (ABPP)
Chairman
Department of Rehabilitation Counseling
Virginia Commonwealth University
Richmond, Virginia

GEORGE HEAD
Help-Line Telephone Clinic
Los Angeles Baptist City Mission Society
Los Angeles, California

MYLDRED E. JONES
Administrative Director
Childrens Hospital Hotline
Los Angeles, California

MICHAEL PECK, Ph.D.
Suicide Prevention Center
Los Angeles, California

HENRY RAYMAKER, Jr., Ph.D.
Chief
Psychology Service
Veterans Administration Center
Dublin, Georgia

CHAPLAIN MEDICUS RENTZ
Help Now
Long Beach Memorial Hospital
Long Beach, California

HY STEINBERG
Director of Education and Training
Texas Youth Council
Austin, Texas

LYNDA STEINBERG
Free Lance Writer
Austin, Texas

PREFACE

Anthropologists have told us that the most persistent institution in the history of mankind is the family unit which has been traced as phenomenon back to the dawn of man. The family has seemed almost impervious to external pressures which threaten it or pressures which impinge upon the individuals within it; however, we are now seeing increased evidence within our culture that the family is not immune to pressure and change. More and more social scientists are confronted with clients whose basic problem is that of the deteriorating family unit. The spectacle of the deteriorating family is depressing. Figures now show that approximately 50 percent of delinquents come from broken homes.

The number of young runaways (some are delinquents, some not) has been estimated to total anywhere from 600,000 to 1,000,000 a year. The recent discovery of the sadistic slayings and secret graves of 27 boys in Houston, Texas, has helped in focusing the much needed attention of parents, professional helping persons, policemen, and others on problems of the teenager who leaves home in what has been called a "runaway." There are many factors involved including rapid social change, the diminishing viability of the family, the self concept of young persons, their search for meaning, problems of rejection and resentment, and the influence of highly influential peer groups and role models.

In this book we have attempted to offer practical information concerning runaway youth and reasons for their behavior as well as helping approaches. We are in great debt to the contributors for without their work this book could have never been developed.

John G. Cull
Richard E. Hardy

Stuarts Draft, Virginia

CONTENTS

Preface

Chapter

PROBLEMS OF RUNAWAY YOUTH

RUNAWAY YOUTH: CAUSES FOR RUNAWAY BEHAVIOR

RICHARD E. HARDY AND JOHN G. CULL

- INTRODUCTION
- REJECTION AND RESENTMENT
- THE SELF-CONCEPT
- IMPORTANCE OF PEER GROUPS AND ROLE MODELS
- RELATIONSHIPS BETWEEN RUNAWAY BEHAVIOR AND DEVELOPMENT TASKS
- SUMMARY

INTRODUCTION

THE RECENT DISCOVERY of the sadistic slayings and secret graves of twenty-seven boys in Houston, Texas, has helped in focusing much needed attention of parents, professional helping persons, policemen and others on problems of the teenager who leaves home in what has been called "runaway." The number of young runaways has been estimated to total anywhere from six hundred thousand to one million a year (Parade Magazine, 1973).

Anthropologists tell us that the most persistent institution in the history of mankind has been the family unit which has been traced as a phenomenon back to the dawn of man. The family has seemed almost impervious to external pressures which threaten it

3

or external pressures which impinge upon the individuals within it; however, we are now seeing increased evidence without our culture that the family is no longer immune to pressure and change. In fact, we are now seeing many types of pressures which are weakening its solidarity. Family disharmony seems on the increase as divorce rates soar, not only in our country and culture but across the world. Perhaps the most persistent attacks on the family unit have centered around questions relating to the effectiveness and purpose of the family. The family now serves a weakened role in inculcating the social and moral values of our society. Other institutions have assumed responsibility for this role and an increased emphasis in molding the opinions and attitudes of young persons has been taken on by their peers. The attacks on the viability and practicality of family units commenced with lower classed families; however, the questions of the efficacy of a family unit have spread to the middle and upper classes so that now it is a generalized concern among sociologists, anthropologists, psychologists and marital counselors.

More and more social scientists are confronted with clients whose basic problem is that of a deteriorating family unit. The spectacle of the deteriorating family is depressing. Figures now show that approximately 50 percent of delinquents come from broken homes, the fact that families are increasingly being broken by desertion and divorce is of immediate concern and even among those family units which remain intact, there are exhibited many problems of a social and emotional nature. Alcoholism, other drug addiction, crime and suicide are now rampant.

The family frequently has been cited as the villain of many social evils but with regard to delinquency and runaway behavior there has been substantial agreement that the family is to blame. The difficult and puzzling stage of adolescence brings about many profound problems. As Mead has aptly stated, "Parents have been rearing unknown children for an unknown world since about 1946" (Mead, 1972).

REJECTION AND RESENTMENT

The rejection of either or both parents by the child or the

parental rejection of the child, is certainly an important factor in demonstrated aggressive behavior on the child's part. Many children feel rejected and react with overt aggression toward parents and the family units. Rejected children generally show a marked tendency toward an increased resistance and quarreling in relationship with adults. They also show considerable sibling rivalry.

Many family members who are confronted with a child's hostile, progressive or delinquent behavior react very negatively. In addition to the problems of financial or social misfortunes, the family as a unit is generally ill prepared to deal with these situations. Often there are real communication problems because there are definite differences in values, especially between the outside peer culture and the individual's family.

There are some early signs which can indicate possibilities for runaway behavior. Some of these include resentment of authority figures in the home and school, resentment of over protection, open conflicts, resentment of discipline, loss of interest in school subjects, impulsivity associated with permissiveness, heavy influence of juvenile peer group, antisocial attitudes, general frustration, involvement with drugs and compensatory behavior.

THE SELF-CONCEPT

It is important for parents and others to understand concepts related to self esteem. Often persons who are prone toward runaway behavior show inadequate self confidence and see themselves in negative ways. An individual who maintains a negative self-concept often continues to behave in accordance with this concept by way of expressing hostility. Counseling sessions with a rehabilitation counselor, social worker, psychologist or other helping profession person can be a real help if this helping individual is keenly tuned into the subculture of youth and current mores and patterns of behavior. Profession service workers and parents must be willing to look into the conditions that produce attitudes leading to runaway behavior. These include the environment of the home and the interrelationships between the individual runaway and his parents and peer associates. Every effort should be made to get children inclined toward this behavior to become involved in meaningful activities, if not possible within their home, at least within their community area. Projects in which students can find meaning through helping others are often of sufficient and substantial value in modifying negative self-concepts and poor attitudes toward the community, home and society in general. If at all possible, families should attempt to have joint projects of mutual interest. These can help in maintaining and improving relationships among family members. Projects should be selected by the family team and not forced upon younger family members by parents or older relatives or siblings.

Another helpful resource is that of grandparents or other relatives who are at least one generation removed from the youth. Since they are less closely associated, there is less ego involvement. Children often can go to such persons and find considerable positive regard and acceptance. In some cases grandparents may be able to be very helpful in that they constantly reinforce positive self-appreciation and more on the part of the young person.

The parent also may wish to consider allowing the young person to get a job in order to become more self-sufficient. This can improve concept of self and cut down on amounts of time which are often used negatively. It should be remembered that most young people get quite bored with themselves, their friends and family units. This is partially due to the large amount of time which many of them use unproductively.

Rapid Social Change and Its Influence on Youth

Institutions such as the church, the family, governmental structures of service, the university, and other educational systems are changing so rapidly that many persons are losing their anchor points for emotional stability. Parents look around them and find little or no certainty in their jobs, in their family life, or in traditional and religious beliefs formerly held sacrosanct. All of us are deeply influenced by the effects of the mass media such as television. These media to us depict what the outside world seems to have. The outside world seems to have so much more than so many think they have.

Diminishing Value of Work

In the early days of the development of this country, the Protestant ethic played a most important part in bringing about advancements in agriculture, technology, and the social service. The amount of hard work which an individual did was a direct indication in many cases of his status in the community. Work for work's sake was highly respected. The Protestant ethic is now much less an influencing factor on attitudes of persons toward work than it once was. In fact, by the year 2000 it may well be that family attitudes in teaching children such characteristics as dependability and diligence related to work may be drastically modified. Society is moving toward a much greater leisure time involvement. At the present time the effects of this accelerating movement away from the Protestant ethic are being felt. This means that convincing persons that the way to success is through hard work of an honest nature is becoming more difficult. Even vocational specialists such as vocational rehabilitation counselors in state and federal agencies are now talking about de-emphasizing vocational aspects of rehabilitation services which in itself indicates some drastic changes in the philosophy of many persons in the social service area on the subject of vocations and work.

There seems to be a definite emphasis toward getting what we want the easy way. This emphasis is perpetuated and reinforced by many white collar workers who are able to "get around the law" by various methods. An example is the landlord who puts enough pressure on tenants to receive monthly payments for rent but does not maintain his buildings according to city ordinances. Youth often see different applications of the law applied according to socioeconomic status of the individual accused. Penalties and sentences can vary enormously according to whether an individual brings an attorney with him to court, whether the offense is a traffic violation or a more serious one. These societal problems greatly influence attitudes of youth.

IMPORTANCE OF PEER GROUPS AND ROLE MODELS

Pressures for conformity come from all sides. Persons in the ghetto feel pressure to conform to the way of behaving of persons of the ghetto. These behavior pressures are particularly strong among the adolescent groups and especially influential among adolescent boys. The emphasis seems to be on beating the "system" somehow, and this attitude should not be considered an unhealthy emphasis. It represents the wish of most Americans—to somehow get established and find happiness within a social system which is now in constant turmoil and within a society which is in many ways unhealthy.

In order for the person from the ghetto, for instance, to beat the system, he must either "fake out" some bureaucratic program such as the Department of Public Welfare and get on the public dole, or behave as two different persons. He must demonstrate one type of behavior which will secure his position within his own peer group and demonstrate another type of behavior which will allow him to secure employment in the outside world. His only other alternative is to leave his peer group and those things which he has felt important in order to enter another man's world. It is much easier for all of us to remain in a world which we have known and adjusted to than it is to modify behavior in order to become members of a different society. Think how difficult it would be for most of us to move into a culture different and distinct from our own. The same types of problems and equal in complexity exist for persons who are from impoverished areas, either rural or urban, when they face finding employment and security in the world of work. These problems cause considerable ambiguity among both parents and youth.

Another problem which often leads to crime and runaway behavior is that of the lack of sufficient role models for individuals to follow. One of the earliest influences on all persons is that of the parents and much of the early child's play involvement is concerned with the work behavior of adults. When adults within the family are not able to work, children closely observe the behavior which they exhibit; this behavior is often characterized by frustration and idleness.

Many youngsters who find themselves in trouble at home need to understand their own motivations—reasons for their behavior. The most prevalent reason, for instance, for difficulty on a job is that of inability to get along with fellow workers. Certainly one of the prime causes of runaway behavior is the inability to get along with others within the family constellation, members of the individual's peer group and members within the community at large. This is often due to personal immaturity. When there is a basic lack of understanding of human nature—the weaknesses and strengths of all of us—there can be a real tendency to misunderstand that behavior which most of us demonstrate most of the time—that of self-centeredness. "Rap sessions" held in various community centers and under the auspices of various community groups may be of substantial value to young persons and to family members also who wish to come into a group situation in order to discuss problems which they may be having. In addition, they will find support and interest in them as individuals which they may have never found before. Many youngsters who exhibit runaway behavior are involved in this type of action in order to gain attention or recognition, having failed in other areas of life in the highly competitive society of today. Quite often runaway behavior is an effort on the youngster's part to have the family stop and take stock of what is happening within the family.

Idleness and hopelessness can be the handmaidens of what has been characterized as "acting out behavior"; that is, the individual is crying for attention, recognition or concern. When youth attempt time and again to find acceptance within their families but can find no point of basic interaction and no acceptance and must remain from their point of view on the outside of a warm interactional relationship within the family, runaway behavior often results. The hopelessness of many youth is profound, especially in ghetto areas where they must sit for hours on porches or in apartments with inadequate facilities and are unable to join in meaningful activity; however, runaway behavior is not the sole province of the ghetto family or the lower socioeconomic class family. Runaway behavior is becoming more and more prevalent among middle-class families and upper class families, especially when the parents become so involved in activities outside the family they are unable to establish warm meaningful relationships with their children. Many youths are unable to find meaningful activities for themselves outside their family constellation. Many youth are just plainly bored. When activity opportunities are lacking and when the ties within the family are weak, chances for runaway behavior and delinquent behavior are compounded.

RELATIONSHIPS BETWEEN RUNAWAY BEHAVIOR AND DEVELOPMENTAL TASKS

Much behavior of individuals can be explained and better understood through the concept of developmental tasks. Havighurst (1957) has outlined the developmental tasks according to age groups of life. He breaks the life span of individuals into six areas: infancy and early childhood, middle childhood, adolescence, early adulthood, middle age, and later maturity. Runaway behavior is generally confined to the period of adolescence which runs from age twelve years to eighteen years. According to Havighurst (1957) there are ten specific tasks within this age frame of adolescence. These are:

1. achieving new and more mature relations with age mates of both sexes.
2. achieving a masculine or feminine social role.
3. accepting one's physique and using the body effectively.
4. achieving emotional independence of parents and other adults.
5. achieving assurance of economic independence.
6. selecting and preparing for an occupation.
7. preparing for marriage and family life.
8. developing intellectual skills and concepts necessary for civic competence.
9. desiring and achieving socially responsible behavior.
10. acquiring a set of values on an ethical system as a guide to behavior.

Many of the causes of runaway behavior among contemporary youth can be tied directly to individual failure of one or more of these developmental tasks of adolescence. Failure to achieve new and more mature relations with age mates leads to a severe social frustration. The individual who failed in this task soon sees that he is out of step with age mates. Successful members of the peer group who are achieving this maturity in their relations with other members of the peer group adjust well and feel more comfortable in social situations; however, the individual who failed in this task feels isolated, alone and has no sense of belonging to the peer group. This is a key factor in precipitating runaway behavior.

Related to the developmental task of achieving new and more mature relations with age mates of both sexes is the task of achieving a masculine or feminine social role. It is at this point that the youngster must assert his identity in the social role and must have a clearly defined self-concept of masculinity or femininity. Again, if he is unable to achieve this level of identity he will be out of step with the peer group and will feel isolated and rejected. The third developmental task is related to the first two but is even more specific in its requirement of adjustment. The third task of accepting one's physique and using the body effectively is a very difficult task for adolescents since this is a period of gangliness and lack of muscular control. Therefore, the individual is clumsy, unfamiliar with his body, unfamiliar with its potential and feels strange with himself and with others. Until he can become adjusted to himself he cannot become adjusted to his peer group.

Perhaps the key developmental task which relates to runaway behavior is the need to achieve emotional independence of parents and other adults. If the individual is not able to achieve a masculine or feminine role and declare himself an adequate, separate, competent individual and sever the emotional ties which have bound him to the parents and have rendered him a child, he will experience extreme frustration. He will feel thwarted in many areas and will feel the only solution to this thwarting and isolation is to escape from the environment. This often results in runaway behavior. •

Runaway behavior can result when the individual feels the requirements of maturity and of "the establishment" impinging on him to the extent he feels socially suffocated. In this situation the individual is striving to retain his immature status and is rejecting the demands for maturity. The few developmental tasks as outlined help to create the drive for runaway behavior in this instance. For example, when the youth who is reluctant to relinquish his maturity is forced to consider achieving economic independence, selecting and preparing for an occupation, preparing for marriage and family life and developing skills and concepts necessary for civic competence, he may feel that if he escapes from the environment he dislikes, he will be able to delay relinquishing the immature role in which he feels so comfortable. Failure on developmental tasks will also provide a clue to predicting runaway behavior. The individual who exhibits runaway behavior totally rejects the developmental tasks of achieving socially responsible behavior. In fact, runaway behavior generally is characterized by socially irresponsible behavior. It is an attempt to reject participation as a responsible adult in the life of the community and the life of the family. However, by rejecting this role, the individual is unable to adequately meet the last developmental task, that of acquiring a set of values and an ethical system as a guide to behavior. For only when an individual is able to function in a socially mature and responsible manner can he get adequate feedback which assists him in developing his own personalized set of values and ethical system which will guide his behavior in a socially responsible manner.

SUMMARY

In summary, runaway behavior is characterized by a panic situation. The young persons feel they must escape from their environment for several reasons; however, all runaways tend to be a crisis situation within the family or within the community. There are pressures on him which are unacceptable and demands which he feels he cannot meet. Therefore, if he runs away he escapes from ·
the reality system which is so unpleasant at either period of time. There often is very little foresight or insightful decision making prior to runaway behavior. If runaway behavior characteristics can be identified by family members or guidance counselors, school teachers, ministers, etc. within the community prior to the decision of the youth to run, counseling can be very effective to solve

the problems. Pressures in the environment which are so unacceptable can be relieved, demands can be eased and the youth can grow and mature socially and psychologically through counseling experiences. If, however, the environment becomes so difficult the individual elects to exhibit runaway behavior, a habit pattern can be developed resulting in an aversion to face up to any hardship.

REFERENCES

Havighurst, R. J.: *Developmental Tasks,* 2nd Ed. New York, Longmans, 1957.

Mead, Margaret: A conversation with Margaret Mead: on the anthropological age. In *Readings in Psychology Today,* Ted. Bell, Mar, California, CRM Books, 1972.

Parade Magazine, October 7, 1973.

SPECIAL PROBLEMS OF THE DELINQUENT GIRL

WILLIAM M. BREER

- THE MODERATELY DELINQUENT GIRL
- DYNAMICS
- THE PRIMARY DEFENSE OF THE DELINQUENT GIRL
- PREGNANCY
- CONTROL, RUNAWAY, AND THE FAMILY
- EGO STRENGTH
- SKIPPING ADOLESCENCE
- CASEWORK WITH THE DELINQUENT GIRL
- HELP FROM THE DELINQUENT GIRL
- BALANCE
- CONTROL AND CASEWORK
- PLACEMENT

THE DELINQUENT GIRL poses a number of serious problems to the caseworker involved in this area. It is a cliché that the female delinquent is harder to work with than her male counterpart. Many practitioners suspect that, like the female alcoholic, the female who violates the societal taboos and becomes delinquent is more disturbed than the delinquent boy. The boy can more easily dally for a while on the wrong side of social mores and not be considered far outside normal limits. When the adolescent girl crosses these same lines, she is considered to be driven by far more pathological inner imperatives. Some of these clichés are highly questionable. Like everything else relating to the female delinquent they are poorly researched. The topic of female delinquency is the preserve of speculation and opinion. Systematic studies are rare if not nonexistent. Any conclusions, including those of this chapter can be little more than tentative.

I had hoped to open this chapter with some neat statistics demonstrating the nature and scope of the problem of the runaway girl. Unfortunately, it cannot be done. Most statistics on runaway behavior are kept by local law enforcement. They are usually lumped in a figure called "missing persons" which, God knows, includes far more than runaway girls. The FBI keeps some figures on minors arrested for runaway, but all runaways are not arrested. To further complicate the statistical picture, a 1963 to 1964 study in Prince George County, Maryland suggested that only one runaway episode in six is actually reported (Shellow, Schamp Liebow, and Unger, 1967, pg. 27). The figures I have been able to gather suggest that in 1969 500,000 young people under seventeen ran from home. Roughly one half of these young people were girls. The trend since 1969 seems to be toward an increase in both the overall number of runaways and the percentage of girls involved (Ambrosino, 1971, pg. 3).

In this chapter I hope to deal with one specific constellation of runaway girls. I must exclude the one time, impulsive runaway because I have little data in this area, and because I feel this type of girl is less likely to be of concern to the caseworker. At the other end of the spectrum, I would exclude the hard core female delinquent who regularly becomes involved in serious criminal behavior. This highly delinquent girl is the one who often ends up in correctional institutions such as the California Youth Authority and is of more concern to the corrections officer than to the caseworker.

This chapter will concentrate on the moderately delinquent girl, the girl whose delinquent behavior is neither a fluke nor part of a pattern of repeated felonious activity. This is the delinquent girl who is most likely to come to the attention of the social agency. My experience and observation suggests that the one time runaway and the confirmed delinquent occupy only the fringes of a continuum, the middle part of which consumes the greater part of the efforts of probation officers, social workers, and family counselors.

The conclusions presented here are drawn from my experience as a probation officer and from an intensive, participant observer study undertaken in the "Girl's Detention Treatment Unit" in order to gather further information for this chapter. The "Girl's Detention Treatment Unit" is a facility of the San Bernardino County Probation Department which accepts delinquent girls for a twenty-one day period of in-custody diagnosis and treatment. Parents are involved in the process and are asked to attend weekly conferences with their daughter and juvenile hall staff. The girls in the program range in age from thirteen to seventeen. Every effort is made to exclude girls who are sophisticated delinquents.

Because of the nature of the data, the tentativeness of these conclusions must be kept in mind. They are in no sense drawn from statistical study or controlled research efforts. They are simply the fruit of personal observation, experimentation, and rumination.

THE MODERATELY DELINQUENT GIRL

When I originally thought about how to present this chapter, I raised the question as to whether it should deal with delinquent girls in general or limit itself to the problems of the runaway girl alone. I quickly came to the conclusion that such a distinction would be hard to make. It is the moderately delinquent girl who is most likely to run away. She is also likely to be involved in a wider pattern of delinquent behavior and attitudes which characterize the moderately delinquent girl in general. For this girl, the act of runaway is part of a larger constellation. She usually shows evidence of severe sexual conflicts which she tries to resolve through promiscuous sexual experimentation. As a result, she often becomes pregnant. The moderately delinquent girl also has severe home problems. She is usually involved in behavior legally defined as "incorrigible"; that is she disobeys, baits, and eludes parental authority.

Some drug experimentation also characterizes the moderately delinquent girl. She is not an addict, but she has most likely used marijuana, alcohol, barbiturates and/or LSD. Sometimes she uses one or more of these drugs regularly and in great quantity. Many of these girls might be viewed as in the early stages of drug dependency. Her attitude about intoxication often reflects the enthusiasm of the recent convert. Such enthusiasm does not characterize the addict. It represents an exhilaration at finding a temporary escape from the emotional turmoil of her adolescence. Later she will learn the drawbacks inherent in this escape.

DYNAMICS

Underlying the behavior of the moderately delinquent girl is a relatively consistent dynamic pattern. These dynamics are complex and have almost infinite individual permutations. To follow these dynamics through all of their intricacies is beyond the scope and intent of this chapter. However, some brief remarks in this area seem essential. In a sense, the underlying dynamics of the delinquent girl are simply an exaggeration of the conflicts that characterize adolescence in general.

One of the most important struggles of the delinquent girl is her conflict between impulses toward maturity and those pushing her back toward a state of childlike dependency. This is really a conflict between growth and regression, the crucial crossroad of adolescence itself. Under the pressure of the hormonal changes of puberty, the old conflicts are reactivated. One course is back toward an infantile dependency upon mother; the other is toward identity as a feminine sexual person and maturity. The delinquent girl sees both paths as fraught with perils and fights both her own impulses and external forces that push in either direction.

A second struggle of the delinquent girl is to free herself from what is often a pathological home situation. Neat classification of these home situations is not possible. In the Detention Treatment Unit, some of the girls had to deal with one or two alcoholic parents, some with physically abusive parents, others with incestuous feelings and advances from fathers, brothers, or other relatives; some were scapegoats; some had come out losers in fierce oedipal competitions.

Many delinquent girls have a strong wish to leave home and live elsewhere. With some it is conscious and unconflicted. With others it is unconscious and ambivalent. The situation is complicated by the fact that often the parents would also like to be rid of their delinquent daughter. The parents' wish may also be unconscious. The roots of such feelings are usually old and deeply buried. It usually generates a great deal of guilt in both parents and child. To parents, the wish to be rid of a child is a transgression of a strong social value, a value so deep it may be rooted in biology. It also represents an acknowledgment of failure in one of the primary tasks of adulthood. For the girl, too, it represents failure. Failure to meet her emotional needs in the most primary setting, the family. It has connotations of being rejected and unlovable. The painful feelings associated with this loss and failure can be overwhelming.

When parents, child, or both have developed a strong drive to separate the girl from the family, the girl is in a painful dilemma. She has two choices, both of which will lead to delinquency. One choice is for the girl to handle feelings of hurt and rage by projection. Her parents become the bad ones. They are her problem. If she can just escape from their home and their control, everything will be all right. Unfortunately, "their control" is often extended to mean escaping from all of the limits set by society. This adjustment to the family crisis has elements of both sociopathy and paranoia. It usually results in a highly delinquent girl.

Another way of handling the problem of separation is for the girl to take the blame for the situation upon herself. She can set out to misbehave so badly that her parents will have to abandon her, and court authorities will be forced to remove her from her home. By doing this, the girl is helping the parents to avoid their own feelings of guilt and failure. She is also dealing with her feelings of rejection and unlovability by engineering a situation in which it is her behavior which has caused her parents to abandon her. The payoff is that she is left with a feeling of control and a defense against unlovability. It was her choice of actions, not her unlovability, which caused her parents to reject her. In this kind of situation, parents may unconsciously encourage the delinquent girl to act out in order to help them escape from feelings of guilt. The girl's delinquency becomes in part a situation of living up to the parents' unconscious expectations. This resolution has strong elements of depression in it. The basic premise is "I'm bad, and it's my fault." In my judgment, this is a more common pattern for the moderately delinquent girl than the parent blaming (sociopathic-paranoid) resolution. It is probably also more treatable.

Discussing feelings about leaving home is usually taboo to the delinquent girl. If she is aware of the desire to leave her family, she feels guilty about it. She also fears the disapproval of adolescent peers. There seem to be strong social pressures operating in groups of adolescent girls to keep them from expressing such feelings, at least in the presence of adults. Occasionally, these resistances break down. In one group in the Girl's Detention Unit, several girls turned their attention to their wish to leave home permanently. Thirteen year old Nancy stated this most clearly with the simple declaration, "I'd rather be here than home." "Here" was a twenty-four hour a day custodial setting with severe restrictions on personal freedoms. Nancy's complaints about home were that her parents blatantly favored a younger brother, and that her father had molested her older sister.

The casual observer will quickly take note of the dependence-independence conflict, the adolescent ambivalence, and the severe home problems of the delinquent girl. Two other problem areas are harder to discern. They are the delinquent girl's fear of homosexuality and her fear of underlying psychosis. One evening in the Detention Treatment Unit, a group of four girls led by Eloise brought up the topic of homosexuality. Without any cue in the preceding conversation, Eloise volunteered, "You get perverted in here. Away from boys all the time, you start to think about girls." The topic thus turned to homosexuality. The girls bombarded me with questions about what was normal. Eloise and Susan both noted that homosexual feelings made them feel "crazy." As the conversation proceeded, it attracted Sandra, a girl known to the others for her avid, promiscuous pursuit of boys and her alleged lack of intelligence. Sandra contributed little but seemed utterly fascinated by the discussion. Perhaps her promiscuity and constriction were defenses against the feelings being discussed by the others.

Delinquent girls usually discuss their fear of psychosis as a fear of "going crazy." These fears are usually carefully concealed. Girls in the Detention Treatment Unit occasionally expressed anxiety about the fact that they were in a treatment unit. They seemed to prefer to identify themselves as delinquents in need of control and punishment rather than crazy people in need of treatment. The fact that they had been singled out for confinement in a treatment unit caused the girls to speculate that the staff felt they were sick. (Who else needs treatment?) This led to vehement declarations that they were not "crazy." This defensiveness is of great importance in dealing with the delinquent girl. She will go to great lengths sometimes to demonstrate that she is delinquent and not disturbed. If this drive cannot be reduced, the moderately delinquent girl can move into the area of serious delinquency and may have to be confined in a correctional institution.

From time to time, the moderately delinquent girl gives verbal hints that she is willing to discuss and work on this underlying problem. Susan, one of the most disturbed girls on the unit, followed her remark that homosexual feelings made her feel crazy with the comment "I'd like to talk to a shrink." Eloise on several occasions verbalized fears that mental illness in her family might be hereditary. Such remarks constitute the girl's permission to the caseworker to help her in an area of significant concern.

THE PRIMARY DEFENSE OF THE DELINQUENT GIRL

Having examined some of the dynamics underlying the behavior of the delinquent girl, let us now consider some aspects of her defense system. I feel that the primary defense of the delinquent girl is control. By this I mean a consistent effort to control the external social environment by a variety of techniques, many of them pathological. This is certainly not the only defense of the delinquent girl, but it is the one of most concern to the caseworker. It is such because it is this drive that gets the delinquent girl into many of the difficulties in which she finds herself. It is also important because unless its roots are understood, the control drive can make it very hard for the caseworker to like the delinquent girl. It thus becomes a barrier to communication and understanding.

I should caution the reader that many of the remarks made here about the delinquent girl may sound like a rejection of her as a person. They are not intended to be so. The control defense is the product of tremendous underlying anxiety. In response to her own inner chaos and the often cruel caprice of her social environment the delinquent girl adopts control in order to reduce her anxieties. If the delinquent girl can obtain some sense of being able to control parents, siblings, peers, and adult authorities outside the family, these forces become a source of far less fear. By defining her problem as the external social environment, the delinquent girl is also able to deal symbolically with her own inner chaos, a problem she knows no other way to handle. Probably it is the inner chaos that is the greater source of anxiety. Her family life may have been terribly pathological, but it often leaves the girl with scars that generate their own terrors. A control drive directed at the external environment permits the girl to externalize her problem. A problem that can be externalized seems far less insolvable than an internal one.

The control drive makes the delinquent girl above all a manipulator. She sets goals toward which all of her efforts and energies are directed. She can cling to these with a single minded intensity. She will center much of her social interaction around realizing these goals. In the Detention Treatment Unit, the goal was to persuade the staff to send you home rather than on to a facility for more extended treatment. I overheard Susan one night as she was explicitly warning some new girls not to talk to the counselors, "They can put you in the G.T.U." (Girl's Treatment Unit, a six month in-custody treatment program).

This situation led to the creation of two tiers of communication in the Detention Treatment Unit, one on which real feelings and attitudes were shared among the girls, and another on which behavior and verbalizations were carefully censored in order to create an impression in the mind of the staff. Girls varied in their ability to maintain this façade in a twenty-four hour a day setting. Some could not hold in their impulses. Others were so ambivalent about home that they shared their conflicts from time to time with the staff. Some were able to behave as "model prisoners" throughout the three week program. One such "model prisoner" ran the day after she was returned home from the program. Another said privately that she would do the same thing if the home situation had not improved when she returned.

Some of the other traits of the delinquent girl are in part techniques for controlling the social environment. Seductiveness is a case in point. The delinquent girl gets full mileage out of her femininity in dealing with men in authority. I doubt that control is the only dynamic behind seductiveness, but it is certainly one of the most important payoffs. The use of seduction as a control technique is probably one of the factors in the promiscuous behavior associated with female delinquency.

PREGNANCY

Pregnancy itself can be a manipulation. It creates severe problems for parents and caseworkers as well as for the delinquent girl. It makes placement difficult, if not impossible. It makes others prone to accept the delinquent girl's premature claims to adult status. It leads families to accept ill conceived marriages as a solution to a crisis. Parents often make dramatic changes in their attitude toward their daughter when she becomes pregnant. Their drive to control her may taper off. Sometimes they adopt a more "live and let live" attitude toward the girl. Sometimes they disown her.

Maria was making plans to get pregnant before her departure from the Detention Treatment Unit. She was to be released to wait at home for placement in the longer term Girl's Treatment Unit. Maria was less than enthusiastic about the plan. In fantasy she had already selected a prospective father for her child. The father was to be a young man for whom she cared very little, but whom she felt would be responsible enough to marry her under the circumstances. If she could make the maneuver work, she could become emancipated from her family, and could appropriate many of the prerogatives of adulthood. Placement would, of course, be out of the question for a married woman with a child.

This does not mean that there are not other reasons for a delinquent girl to become pregnant. The primary causes probably lie in the unconscious. Such deeply concealed motivations are hard to verify. They are certainly beyond the scope of this chapter. At the other end of the spectrum of motivation, a pregnancy can, of course, be the result of lack of caution and the inability to obtain and use birth control devices. The point stressed here, however, is the manipulative advantage that can come from a pregnancy. These advantages can lead either to a deliberately sought pregnancy or enough ambivalence about the idea that active steps are not taken to prevent one.

CONTROL, RUNAWAY, AND THE FAMILY

One interpretation of the frequently strong drive to return to a pathological home is that the delinquent girl has psyched out her parents to such a degree that she can enjoy a feeling of considerable control in the home situation even if she must also endure feelings of rejection and exploitation. In family situations involving adolescent delinquency, male or female, careful analysis often suggests that it is the adolescent who has the preponderance of control of the family situation.

The act of running away from home can be a way of gaining this control. Many parents respond with guilt and critical introspection to a runaway episode. They frequently conclude that they are to blame for the problem and resolve to make changes. Unfortunately, this often leads to an excess in the opposite direction. The result may be a near abdication by the parent and a child in the home with few limits on her behavior. In the long run, this is highly destructive to the adolescent.

EGO STRENGTH

Implicit in the remarks made so far is the generally weak ego development of the delinquent girl. Her overdeveloped need to control others is suggestive of a lack of confidence in her own ego functioning. Some of the literature and research in this area suggest that weakness of the ego may reflect the delinquent girl's poor ability to handle underlying psychotic processes. Leventhal makes this point clearly in a 1963 article:

> On the basis of the marked overconcern with the loss of control and with ego surrender, and some degree of reality distortion, prepsychotic functioning is suggested. In this connection it is interesting to note that a recent follow up study of cases referred to child guidance clinics, the runaways were one of the groups most likely to show psychotic reactions as adults (Levanthal, 1963, pg. 127).

Leventhal is writing of runaways in general, but his point seems quite relevant to the subject of this chapter.

I do not wish to belabor or inflate this point, but it is interesting in view of the fears of "going crazy" verbalized in the Detention Treatment Unit. This is an area needing further research before definitive statements can be made. In final reference to this subject, we might note that becoming psychotic is also a form of running away. The delinquent girl runs outward, the psychotic girl runs inward.

SKIPPING ADOLESCENCE

The delinquent girl often gives the impression that she is trying to grow up all at once, to move directly from latency to adulthood, magically skipping the turmoil of adolescence. The girls in the Detention Treatment Unit have an almost frantic need to be worldly and sophisticated. The worst *faux pas* in the peer group is to be naïve. The girls talk with great enthusiasm about their adventures on the run, the boyfriends they had met, their promiscuous relationships, and their use of drugs. To be an adult seems to mean delinquency and familiarity with the seamy side of life. Not to be so familiar is to be a baby. The underground world of the runaway and delinquent represent the pinnacle of sophistication to the girls in the Detention Treatment Unit.

CASEWORK WITH THE DELINQUENT GIRL

We have explored some of the personality patterns of the delinquent girl. We might now profitably turn our attention to using this information to help the delinquent girl deal with her problems. The most important concept is that a careful evaluation of the individual girl and her problems is an essential concept of departure. Different degrees of pathology are manifested in the symptom of runaway behavior. Running from home can range from a symptom of relatively mild disturbance to one of severe pathology. Some girls who run away are schizophrenic. Severe symptoms, even overt hallucinatory and delusional experiences, sometimes go undetected. Lesser pathology runs an even greater risk of going undetected. Once a careful diagnostic evaluation has been made, casework can begin. The precise nature of the treatment will depend upon the evaluation. There are, however, some constant features of casework with the delinquent girl that spring from the general nature of the problems, and which will be useful in most situations.

HELP FROM THE DELINQUENT GIRL

Perhaps the greatest tool in working with the delinquent girl is her own ambivalence. She may resent limits and adults who impose them, but she also knows that without limits her behavior may get totally out of control and she will find herself in deep trouble. The delinquent girl will usually offer a number of verbal cues to those around her allowing them to anticipate her acting out. This seems to be a way of asking adults to set limits. Two examples come to mind.

Several girls in the Detention Treatment Unit, led by Darla, came up with an escape scheme which involved hitting the night lady over the head with a mop and taking her key. Darla did not

seem like a severely delinquent girl. The plan was poorly worked
out and impractical. Before it was to be implemented, Darla
talked about it so much that word spread through the grapevine,
and everyone in the unit knew of the plan. Darla then brought
the scheme up with her counselor. The discussion, of course,
forced the girls to abandon the plan. It appears that Darla was
asking that limits be set to prohibit her from an act of physical
violence and an escape from juvenile hall that would have gotten
her into far more trouble than she was already in. If there were
no ambivalence about the scheme, it is doubtful that Darla would
have fed it into the grapevine or discussed it with her counselor.

Ann Applebaum, writing in a 1960 anthology on adolescence,
sites a more dramatic example. She was attempting to treat a
schizophrenic girl by means of psychotherapy in an inpatient
setting. The girl's behavior toward the therapist was verbally
abusive and physically menacing. She would, however, give the
therapist curiously reversed cues on how to restrain her, such as,
"Don't you dare hold my hands, then I can't fight." Meaningful
treatment began when the therapist took these cues and physically
restrained the girl during the therapeutic sessions.

The meaning of this girl's need to be physically restrained
seems to be that she was so preoccupied with her violent, out
of control behavior that no verbal treatment could begin until
she felt her therapist was strong enough to set limits on her
physical behavior. Admittedly, this girl is more disturbed than
most of the runaway delinquents that will be dealt with in general
casework situations. The difference is, however, in some ways
quantitative rather than qualitative. The delinquent girl also has
fears that her behavior will go out of control. She, too, will
cooperate in the setting of limits.

A second way the delinquent girl helps the caseworker is with
her need to communicate and be understood. On the surface,
delinquent girls maintain a façade of alienation and disinterest
in adults. Girls in the Detention Treatment Unit repeatedly
complained that adults do not listen to teen-agers, and that therefore they do not understand them. Beneath this façade, the girls
are looking for adults with whom they can communicate and,
hopefully, identify. Much of their reluctance to communicate is

really fear of further rejection from the adult world. The delinquent girl will test the adult to see if he can listen and understand without rejecting. If the adult passes the test, he will be amazed at the information that pours forth.

It is in this area of ambivalence and implicit cooperation with the caseworker that the moderately delinquent girl differs most markedly from the girl who is severely delinquent. As she becomes more delinquent, a girl's struggle against limits becomes less conflicted, and she more and more shuts adults out of her world. At the end of the continuum, the caseworker has little with which to work.

BALANCE

In working with the delinquent girl, the caseworker must strive for a balance between empathy and understanding on the one hand and limit setting on the other. It is essential to keep in mind the highly manipulative nature of the delinquent girl and her strong drive to control others. If this is not attended to, the caseworker will be exploited and manipulated by the girl. She will ultimately regard him as a patsy who cannot really help. On the other hand, we need to remember that the delinquent girl uses her defenses in response to problems in her own development which she has been unable to cope with in any other way.

Some of the complaints of the delinquent girl will be legitimate. She may have been treated unfairly by parents, schools, or law enforcement agencies. Feelings springing from these legitimate complaints should be respected. If there is no remedy, they should be dealt with as unpleasant realities with which all human beings must learn to deal. On the other side of the coin, the caseworker should work with parents and others with authority roles to set firm and fair limits within which the delinquent girl must function. The adult should stress that he will do everything in his power to see that the girl stays within such limits. To do this well is to steer a course between the Scylla of arbitrary control and the Charybdis of permissiveness, a difficult task for anyone.

CONTROL AND CASEWORK

The issue of who is to control is a difficult one in dealing with the delinquent girl. An important part of this issue is how much of a role in making decisions about her life should be given to the delinquent girl. Casework orthodoxies range from giving the "client" almost complete control to practically none. In my judgment, the basic ground rule should be to give the girl as much control of the situation as is possible within the limits of reality. The relative maturity, responsibility, age, and intelligence of the girl will be important factors in the final equation. The specific role of the caseworker such as probation officer, social worker, or family therapist will also have to be taken into account. Each of these roles has demands and responsibilites effecting the latitude that can be given the delinquent girl in decision making.

This issue needs to be stressed because delinquent girls are so concerned with the question of control. If all sense of control over their lives is taken from them, they can become sullen, rebellious, and self-destructive. The issue is in part a bogus one since the delinquent girl really has a veto power over any plan devised by a caseworker. If she fights a plan deviously enough and with sufficient determination, she can usually render it ineffective. On the other hand, if she has a sense of participation, she is more likely to develop one of cooperation. Freedom and responsibility within the framework of reality also helps to prepare the delinquent girl for adulthood. Rather than hope to impose change where there is no hope of change, we need to learn where there are ambivalences and to come down firmly on the side of mental health and better functioning.

PLACEMENT

It seems appropriate to end this chapter with some comments on the caseworker's last resort, placement. A part of the ongoing process of dealing with the delinquent girl should be a careful evaluation of whether her home has sufficient strengths for her to continue to live there. Many girls are returned to hopelessly pathogenic homes. A great deal of casework is expended trying to treat families which are untreatable as an intact unit. We need to recognize a hopeless situation and give up on it if this is the case. Usually the delinquent girl will give ample cues that she is unable to deal with the reality of her home. The risk involved in returning her to an untreatable home is that it will drive her to greater and greater delinquencies with the unconscious goal of forcing the caseworker to remove her from the situation.

REFERENCES

Below are some of the references I have found useful in understanding the problems of the delinquent girl. This is in no sense offered as a comprehensive listing of the literature on the topic. The works included represent differing theoretical and practical approaches to the problem of the delinquent girl.

Ambrosino, Lillian: *Runaways.* Boston, Beacon Press, 1971.
This little book is a kind of pop approach to the problem of runaway children in general. It provides basic information on the legal and practical problems faced by the child on the run. Its main value is its suggestions for coping with the immediate crisis situation resulting from the runaway episode.

Applebaum, Ann Wilkin: The meaning of external control to a schizophrenic adolescent girl. In Sediman, Jerome M. (Ed.): *The Adolescent, A Book of Readings.* New York, Holt, Rinehart, and Winston, 1960.
This article is of interest in that it puts the need for external limits into very strong relief. The case is extreme, but it has analogies in dealing with the delinquent girl.

Erikson, Erik H.: *Identity, Youth, and Crisis.* New York, Norton, 1968.
This is an excellent general work for those dealing with young people. The chapter "Womanhood and Inner Space" should be read by anyone who wants to understand and deal meaningfully with the problems of the delinquent girl.

Konopka, Gisela: *The Adolescent Girl in Conflict.* Englewood Cliffs, Prentice-Hall, 1966.
This work is based on a participant observer study in a facility for delinquent girls in Minnesota. The study was prolonged and intensive. Conclusions are sensitively drawn by the author who is an experienced caseworker. The girls involved are severely delinquent, but the author presents them in such a way that they emerge as human beings in trouble rather than as "cases" or inmates.

Leventhal, T.: Control problems in runaway children. *Archives of General Psychiatry*. Vol. 9 No. 2, pp 122–26, 1963.

This is an excellent theoretical treatment of the role of control in the dynamics of the runaway.

Meyer, Henry J., Borgatta, Edgar, and Jones, Wyatt C.: *Girls at Vocational High*. New York, Russell Sage Foundation, 1965.

This is a carefully documented study of a group of girls with actual or incipient problems at a school in New York City. An experimental group was referred to a nearby social agency. A control group was not treated. No measure available in the school setting suggested a significant difference between the treated and untreated groups. These findings can be challenged on several grounds, but anyone interested in casework should be aware of this study and its implications.

Pollak, Otto, and Friedman, Alfred S. (Eds.): *Family Dynamics and Female Sexual Delinquency*. Palo Alto, Science and Behavior Books, 1969.

This is a collection of articles discussing the underlying dynamics of the delinquent girl and her family. Most of the contributors are therapists involved directly in the treatment of such families. This is probably the best exploration of the unconscious structures and family dynamics that underlie the acting out of the delinquent girl.

Shellow, R., Schamp, J. R., and Unger, E.: Suburban runaways of the 1960's. In *Monographs of the Society for Research in Child Development*. Vol. 32. No. 3, 1967. University of Chicago Press.

This is a sociological study of runaway children in Prince Georges County, Maryland. It presents some provocative statistics. It is, however, based on a limited sample in a limited greographical area. The authors draw a number of psychological conclusions. In general, the conclusions of this study seem questionable. This is partly because of the nature of the sample and partly because of the unsoundness of making psychological inferences from sociological data and techniques.

Weintreb, J., and Counts, R.: Impulsivity in adolescents and its therapeutic management. *Archives of General Psychiatry*. Vol. 2. No. 5. pp. 548–58, 1960.

This article offers some excellent suggestions for dealing with the delinquent child in a psycho-therapeutic setting. Unfortunately, these suggestions are very difficult to incorporate into a more superficial casework and management situation. The article is worth reading and a synthesis of these suggestions and casework is worth attempting.

PROBLEMS OF THE RUNAWAY BOY

Hy Steinberg and Lynda Steinberg

- GOING ON THE RUN: WHY?
- ON THE RUN: PROBLEMS
- DEVELOPMENTAL DISARRAY
- A MODEL
- A PROPOSAL FOR TREATMENT: PHASE I
- CONCLUSION

GOING ON THE RUN: WHY?

HE, LIKE THOUSANDS of others, takes to the road each month. If we are to understand the "why" of it, then we must listen to him. The boy who has left home without his parents' knowledge or permission might tell us that his parents did not understand him. This is too general to enlighten us; further probing might yield such complaints as parental criticism which was too often directed at the boy. Or, that the parents didn't trust him, that they were always asking where he was going and with whom, and for how long or for what purpose.

Some boys complain that their parents disliked their friends or decried their taste in music, clothing, grooming, reading, etc.

Others tell of their parents' demonstrable disappointment in the way that they are turning out; that they nag, criticize, and pressure them to change. The boys charge that they are compared to other supposedly exemplary boys and that their parents are prone to misinterpretation of the motives for much of their behavior. Where drug taking is involved, the parents are seen as incapable of understanding since they are straight themselves.

Some parents are accused of making demands that the child deems unreasonable. Others are said to vacillate from the permissive to the strict end of a discipline continuum, with no systematic reason for doing so. Yet others seem set upon molding their child into some very specific form. Infantile and overprotective treatment is called a cause as often as is the application of overbearing pressure and the assignment of heavy responsibilities to the child.

Some boys lodge much more serious complaints against their parents ranging from alcoholism, brutality between each other or directed at the child, parental promiscuity, sexual assault, deliberate mental cruelty or extreme favoritism to other siblings, any of which results in an environment which is intolerable to the child. There are kids who say they are simply running away from the so-called hypocrisy of the middle-class parental life-style or to seek adventure which they don't seem to be able to find on the home scene.

How might we sum all of this up and draw a conclusion? The runaway may feel that it is his deficit alone which causes such negative responses from his parents. Or he may feel that it is their deficit alone which forces him to run away from such unhappy circumstances. For others, leaving home may be a dire necessity; things may just be too bad to stay, yet running away is not necessarily the desirable solution. In all cases the parents are not communicating appropriately with their children, nor the children with them. The problems of some might appear to be less serious than those of others. Yet for each individual, his troubles or needs have overwhelmed him in his present circumstances and he takes the runaway route away from them. Where shall he go and what shall he do?

ON THE RUN: PROBLEMS

The runaway boy faces a multitude of difficulties once he has left home. The first and most pressing of these are the ones which relate to survival. Having forsaken the comfort and provisions of the home hearth, he must now seek out and procure his own food, clothing, shelter, transportation, and income. He is further placed in physical danger through his increased proximity to areas where crime rates are high (many runaways head for large metropolitan inner-city neighborhoods when they run) and through increased exposure to drugs, unclean living conditions, venereal diseases, hepatitus, kidney and bladder infections, infectious respiratory illnesses, borderline malnutrition, foot injuries and cuts due to lack of proper footgear. Consider too, the entire gamut of dental problems which arise out of poor nutrition, lack of professional care, and inadequate cleanliness.

In order to meet his survival needs, the runaway boy—who is most usually not a delinquent prior to running—must resort to commiting criminal or anti-social acts. In the first place, running away is considered a crime. The boy is liable to arrest for being absent from home for more than 24 hours without parental permission. Anyone who gives aid to the runaway without reporting him or having him contact his parents, can be considered to have abetted a delinquent. With such a law on the books and being enforced, he who would help the runaway has an obstacle in his path. If the runaway cannot be convinced to call home and obtain permission to remain with his would-be helper, then the helper cannot keep him under his roof at night without risking arrest.

While it can be understood how such a law protects the rights of the runaway's parents and while it may often be in the best interest of the runaway himself, it would still make sense to modify or amend the law so that it would not force determined or fearful runaway youth away from sources of help simply because they would not call home. If the law stands as it is presently, halfway houses cannot help the many youth who will not ask for or may not receive permission from their parents to remain. They are forced to take to the street once again.

While the runaway may be able to stay with generous friends

for a time, he will sooner or later have to provide for himself. For food, clothing, and patent medicine, he may panhandle, (a dead give-away to his runaway status) he may work (highly unlikely if he is under 18 and must produce working papers) or he may shop-lift. The high frequency with which he may need to steal in order to live, places him in almost constant danger of arrest.

Without access to his father's car and with no ready cash for public transportation, the runaway is a frequent hitch-hiker, and in many states this is illegal. He doesn't always have a place to spend the night and so the runaway is vulnerable to detention for loitering, sleeping in public buildings or for being wayward.

In short, the runaway stands a good chance of being arrested. Once he has been picked up by the police he may be referred to a juvenile home. If his experiences as a wayward youth have not already left him jaded, then his stay in the juvenile home will likely do the trick.

Thrust in among the hard core delinquents, he faces all of the violence, the mistreatment, and other negative experiences which characterize most penal institutions. He will be used by some in-mates, abused by others, or perhaps, if he hits it off, taught the ropes. He will undoubtedly be changed by his stay.

The runaway may have managed to rid himself of the specific people and problems which made him uptight, but he has im-mersed himself in a street culture or a penal culture which will quickly erect a total new environment of difficulties. He will learn to mistrust people even more than previously. He has learned about fear; of the street and its inhabitants or of the juvenile home and its concomitant horrors.

He doesn't find solutions. There are few "together" people to emulate. Instead, he encounters merely false relationships with others and these usually end in disappointment. He is most likely to be rubbing elbows with full-time drifters, petty criminals, drug pushers, junkies, prostitutes and other kids on the run, along with a number of pathetic or unsavory individuals who live a marginal existence as a result of failure to make it in the real world. Shelters such as urban Y.M.C.A.'s or fleabag hotels and cheap rental rooms are inhabited by a fair number of alcoholics, misfits, debilitated persons or former mental patients who are no longer tolerated by their families.

Running has simply brought the runaway up short. He is at the end of the line. He feels disappointment that he is still dissatisfied and unfulfilled. He is uncomfortable in his surroundings, and is feeling remorseful for causing his family grief and worry. He is desperate for another solution.

He often chooses to return home, despite the consequences and the fact that he is going home to a troublesome situation. Or he may continue to drift along as is. Whichever he chooses, he still has a heavy burden to bear and he has acquired no new skills to help him handle it.

DEVELOPMENTAL DISARRAY

What has gone awry in the development of the runaway child? How has he arrived at this point in time which finds him far from the source of his primal nourishment, yet equidistant from any true and meaningful self-realization and self-stimulated growth?

An infant is prepared for the future by his caring mother and father. They attend to his physical needs by nursing, bathing, dressing, and holding him and this appropriate tending affords him the security he needs to have in an environment in which he cannot survive by himself. Most parents also attend to his psychological needs by loving him and guiding him. The parents form the largest part of the boy's environment and so are always present as models of the kind of behavior and growth they expect from him. If they have found their own lives' direction and have been able to relate to the world in a way which is distinctively theirs and which works for them, then they are effective persons. It is upon this base of their effectiveness and growthful success that parents must build their own efforts to facilitate a child's growth. The parent wants to and intends to guide his child and to help him develop by teaching him all about living and about what he has found to work in his own life. It is possible to say that the more effective the parent, then the more effective the responses he will have in his own bag to pull out and present, through modeling and teaching, to his child. The converse is just as sure. If the parent is not effective in his own life then he will have fewer "gifts" (skills) to present to his child. With a half-full chest of life's tools to bequeath to his children, he will be much less potent than his counterpart, the parent with a full set of tools. When the parent needs to use, for example, a level and finds that there is none in his chest, then he must get by with an uneven foundation. The building will be shakier as a result.

"Responsive behavior is one of the basic dimensions of child-rearing," and "initiative behavior is the other basic dimension of child-rearing" (Carkhuff, 1972).

If a parent is to be effective, he must be able to respond to his child's needs, feelings, and behavior. He must guide and direct the child by drawing upon the resources of his own experiences. If he cannot both respond and initiate with his child, then he will not be readily distinguishable (behavior-wise) from the child. What will he have to offer if he hasn't the ability to respond and initiate?

The child whose parents can demonstrate an ability to hear what he says, to be responsive to what he says and to aim him toward the growth he needs will want to try out that very behavior for himself. Of course, when he does experiment with it he will find that it works, it gets him to where he wants to be.

If the child has not had positive behavior demonstrated for him, he is at a disadvantage. He too will try out the behavior his parents have modeled. Chances are it will not get him where he wants to go just as it didn't work well for his parents. But it is all they knew and it is all they had to offer him. He may want to reject the behavior and try something else, but what? Some searching children run away to escape what never worked for them.

Surely, the key to unblocked development in the young is that they receive fully the basic dimensions of human development. If the dimensions aren't given, then the development is blocked.

A MODEL

Having considered some causes for running and having confronted the problems which spring up about the runaway we must now turn one more corner and consider a way of attacking the problem which is interpersonal skills inadequacy. The solution is interpersonal skills training for kids and parents.

Our choice is a model for helping runaways which will lead to changed behavior and provide the runaway with better ways of dealing with his own needs and growth. We have chosen Carkhuff's Human Resource Development model and intend to show how it might be integrated into a workable network of Runaway Residential Centers which would identify, contact and contract to train runaways and which would return them, with constructive programs and new skills to their old communities or homes.

Carkhuff has identified three goals of helping: self-exploration, self-understanding, and constructive action (Carkhuff, 1972). It is with these goals in mind, and with the overall goal of increasing the quality and quantity of the runaway's skills, that we intend to demonstrate the efficacy of the Carkhuff model as it would function as a deterrent to runaways, providing them with other ways of handling their problems (screening out, predicting, training). But mostly, as it would be a helping model, after-the fact; a helping model for training runaway youth so that they will not have to live on the run, but can map out other, more constructive courses of action.

Throughout this discussion, please keep in mind that there can be no program or model that is any better than the person who writes or implements it. Only people who are productive (which simply means that they work hard with what skills they have) can make this model work.

Remember too that a process must yield productive outcome for the population being treated or trained. A delivery system is needed where the process (training) leads to the desired outcome (changed behavior that is growthful and in no way dependent upon fugitive, anti-social, or self-destructive behavior).

A PROPOSAL FOR TREATMENT: PHASE I

The Runaway Residential Center

A Runaway Residential Center (RRC) should be simply a place

where runaways can come for help and incidentally be provided with food and shelter if they agree to live up to the certain conditions set for them. An RRC would send out a liaison man to reach runaways in the community. Such an out-reach extension would search the street, the hang-out, the park and the police station, salvation army, or any other agency which might draw runaway boys to it. The out-reach worker would approach a boy and establish a relationship with him based upon the out reacher's ability to respond to the boy and further, his authority to offer temporary room and board. In the cases where runaways have been picked up on vagrancy charges or on charges of survival-related crimes, the apprehending agency might arrange to have the boy transferred to the RRC. This would avoid incarceration. Such a suggestion is highly tentative and dependent not only upon the re-writing of certain runaway laws, but also upon the strength of the relationship which exists between the RRC and local law enforcement.

Once the runaway enters the RRC, several things may happen. First, he will have his physical needs attended to: food, clothing, a shave, first aid, sleep if he needs it. As soon as possible, he will be assigned to a "helper-worker" staff member who will orient him to house rules and extend the relationship already begun by the outreach worker. As the "helper-worker" and the boy talk about the boy's problems and the RRC Program, it becomes apparent that the "helper-worker" can be trusted because he seems to understand just how the boy feels and just what he needs at this time. In most cases, the boy will conclude that he needs to remain at the RRC, where he is being offered training. The "helper-worker" tells him the training will teach him how to find the better life and make the better world which has so far eluded him. If he accepts the conditions put to him, then he will live at the RRC and receive training until he is equipped to move on to where he wants or needs to be (home, a foster home, or self-sufficiency).

During Phase II of this tripartite program, an assessment of the boy is made. He will be evaluated in terms of his physical (P), intellectual (I), and emotional (E) functioning. Once the facts about him are known, the teaching of Interpersonal Skills is begun along with training in the "P" and "I" areas. The final stages of Phase II are devoted to the teaching of problem-solving and problem development skills.

The goal of teaching the program development skills is to provide the boy with a way to build success into anything he does. The effectiveness of his programs will be a function of their detail. As he learns the deep satisfaction of succeeding, his behavior begins to modify so that success is generalized from himself to others: friends, family, co-workers, and community members. In other words, as the boy begins to feel that he is worthwhile, he becomes free to contribute to others.

Before long, the boy in training understands that effective work is totally dependent upon his input, his programs and his organizational designs. When skill development becomes a way of life for him, the boy will emerge as a model for other boys and will contribute to their success as well as his own.

In very concrete terms, what Phase II means is that the runaway, once he has (with help) decided to meet our conditions (receive training), will stay on at the RRC. He will attend Interpersonal Skills classes, physical exercise and activity sessions, and academic classes which pick him up where he left off. When he has reached a point of minimal effectiveness in these areas, he will be ready to go home or to develop some other constructive alternative for himself. While most boys will opt for home, anxious to try out their new skills and improve upon the old life, others will not want to return to conditions which they still see (even after training) as hopelessly bad.

Phase III is the Exit Program. An Exit Program is a systematic way of continuing the boy's P.I.E. programs after he leaves RRC. A boy with an exit program will be able to carry his benefits back into the world he left behind. Such a program will ease his re-entry and will have transfer value to his family and friends.

The ultimate goal of the Exit Program is to provide the boy with a fulfilling P.I.E. program that will eliminate his need to run away again or to re-engage in anti-social behavior. With it he will have a means of coping with the change in his environment.

Having alternatives to runaway behavior, which encourage growth and fulfillment, is essential to the betterment of the runaway boy and to society. Without planned prerogatives to exercise, the boy is likely to slip back into his old ineffective ways of doing things.

Having generally described all three phases of the program, it is necessary now to enlarge upon the core, that is, the Skills Training and the trainers themselves. The heart of the RRC is this training and the major emphasis is on raising the boy's interpersonal level of functioning, with proportional gains intellectually and physically. This is accomplished through disciplined, structured training experiences with work as the process and increased productivity as the outcome. As the boy gains insights into his emotional problems, he is freed up to thrust in other areas. His new skills give him the confidence and desire to attempt things never before thought possible. The boy has a new set of responses in four critical areas of all interpersonal relationships.

(1) He can attend by listening, looking, observing, visually evaluating, paying attention to, instilling visual confidence and hope in another, making him feel as if he is the only other person in the world and that he places supreme importance upon what he has to communicate to him.

(2) He can respond; he can tell himself or another exactly the way they feel (as they have already expressed it) and why they feel that way.

(3) He can discriminate by recognizing how another person feels or he can recognize an effective response.

(4) He can initiate by summing up what he says to himself or what another says and find common themes which are contributory factors to his problems. Further, he is able to confront himself on inconsistencies and incongruencies in order to fully involve himself in a growth process.

With these skills, the boy is armed with practical devices for exploring his problems and his world. Equipping him with concrete, measurable skills increases his chance for success and enhances his impact on society.

The trainers who staff the RRC are crucial; without them there is no program. They are the surrogate parents, the solid models for searching youth, the guides to the future. It is important to describe briefly, therefore, the process by which they are selected.

Five criteria are used: 1) resume evaluation, 2) an inventory of their physical, intellectual, and emotional functioning, 3) an evaluation of responses to a standardized tape of critical incidents in the lives of typical runaways, 4) an evaluation of potential as seen during a selection interview, 5) an evaluation of functioning in interpersonal skills training.

In each area (P.I.E.) the candidate may be rated from 1.0 (least effective) to 5.0 (most effective) with 3.0 being minimally effective. Selecting in this systematic and measurable way insures the potential trainer will be functioning at high levels in the areas in which he will be training. This insures that he will be most likely to succeed. Without such a selection procedure, the person selected to act as surrogate parent, model, and potent reinforcer, just might turn out to be a loser. Losers cannot help other losers!

An effective trainer-parent model introduces himself as an important person. While he need not dress in a fashion which might turn off the boys, he should groom himself properly and use clothing as clothing rather than as a prop for his own performance. He projects a high energy level and is capable of providing direction by establishing a substantive base with the boys. He must demonstrate to them that there is room for them there and respond to them in such a way that they will feel that they belong.

He will define his goals, set limits, establish himself as a potent force in the lives of his trainees. He will show initiative early and with the strongest of the boys so that he will be more readily accepted. He will keep his trainees working if he wants them to learn. He will teach and model discipline and structure for them, and set up conditions for success. He is a winner.

CONCLUSION

For the boy who travels through all phases of our R.R.C. program, the prognosis is success. He will leave the possessor of new skills in the interpersonal area; ways of responding to himself and those around him. These ways will give him the power to influence himself and others positively. He will leave in better physical condition. His cardio-vascular functioning will have improved, thus, also his energy level and will have the endurance for doing what he will want and need to do. He will not tire as easily, will have greater physical motivation to get things done. He will look better, healthier complected, and have improved muscle tone. Perhaps he will have lost or gained weight, whatever his need and his program dictated. If so, he will carry away with him a new confidence in his amended self.

Among his other possessions will be new study skills for formal academic work or for his informal intellectual program. In either case, his efforts will mean more to him when they result in greater understanding and retention.

The most critical thing he will carry away from the RRC as proof of his stay there will be his exit program. If he follows it, he will continue to grow and function at ever higher levels.

The boy will have travelled a long way from his unfulfilling home experiences. That road was likely one that wound from bad to worse and then to the excitement of discovery. The RRC is a journey through a variety of people, programs, and an organization that leads to the fullness of human potential and growth.

This entire proposal is intended to remedy the predicament of the runaway boy. It is a sound program and one which will have good results since it teaches, models, and builds in success. It is feasible and such programs have already been used with juvenile delinquents (Patch, *et. al.* 1971) and hard-core adult convicts and jail inmates (Devine, *et. al.* 1974). The results, to date, have been dramatic.

But what about reversal of this critical runaway trend. Would it not make the most sense to utilize the huge public school network as a means of training students, teachers, and parents and as a vehicle for identifying and treating potential runaways.

Academic deterioration, one smoke signal sent up by the future runaway, is often noticed first at school. If teachers are trained in the responsive and initiative skills then they can write their own programs for treatment via training. In this way, also, parents might receive training which was school based and offered as a community resource and service. With both parents and children attending, responding and initiating with one another, there need be no communication breakdown, but rather a reinforcement of understanding, commitment to solution, and action.

The number of yearly runaways has been estimated at up to one million. If we consider, further, the high incidence of divorce and desertion along with the fact that nearly one half of all United States hospital beds are occupied by patients with emotional problems, then we must not merely justify our call for training, we must insist upon it absolutely.

REFERENCES

Ambrosino, L.: *Runaways.* Boston, Beacon Press, 1971.

Carkhuff, Robert R.: *The Art of Helping.* Amherst, Human Development Press, 1972.

———: *The Art of Problem Solving.* Amherst, Human Development Press, 1973.

———: *Development of Human Resources.* Amherst, Human Development Press, 1971.

———: *Helping and Human Relations.* New York, HR&W, 1969, Vol. I.

———: *Helping and Human Relations.* New York, HR&W, 1969, Vol. II.

———: *Sources of Gain in Counseling and Psychotherapy.* New York, HR&W, 1967.

———, and Berenson, B. G.: *Beyond Counseling and Therapy.* New York, HR&W, 1967.

Devine, Joseph P., Steinberg, H., and Bellingham, R.: *First Annual Report Community Based Treatment Program, County of Kalamazoo,* unpublished report, 1974.

Patch, W., Steinberg, H., and Keeling, T.: *Indices of Growth,* unpublished research, Rhode Island Training School for Boys, 1971.

Steinberg, H., and Bellingham, R.: *Selection and Training As The Art of Delivery* (Unpublished Training Manual), Kalamazoo Law Enforcement Facility, 1973.

Wein, B.: *The Runaway Generation.* New York, McKay, 1970.

SPECIAL PROBLEMS OF GAY RUNAWAYS

David L. Aiken

- PARENTS
- PEERS
- SELF-IMAGE
- COUNSELING APPROACHES

O NE OUT OF TEN, and probably more, of the runaways on the streets of America's cities and the highways leading to them are homosexual.

Yet some counselors and others in the business of helping runaways remain unaware of this segment of the runaway population. Asked how many gay young people they counseled, some say none. It is statistically likely that there have been several, whether they know it or not.

There are many reasons for this lack of awareness on the part of some counselors; it's not merely an inability to detect some kind of tell-tale signs. More often, it is a simple lack of knowledge about, contact with and sensitivity toward gay people on the part of heterosexual, or "straight" counselors.

Such counselors have little idea what it's like to grow up gay in a world that's not only straight but often very narrow. Gay young people share many experiences and problems with their straight peers, but they also have a special set of experiences and problems that set them a little bit apart.

This chapter will attempt, in a necessarily cursory and basic way, to describe some of the special problems of growing up gay. These are treated under the headings of problems with parents, problems with peers, and problems with self-concept, although of course all are related. We will then offer some suggestions for counselors who wish to increase their effectiveness with gay youth, and list some resources for those who wish to pursue the topic further or who are confronted with particular cases and need help coping.

First, however, a word about statistics and definitions. There is a lot of loose talk about homosexuality that needs to be cleared away before serious discussion can begin.

The estimate that 10 percent of runaways are gay is an extrapolation from the Kinsey Report (*Sexual Behavior in the Human Male,* by Alfred C. Kinsey, Wardell B. Pomeroy and Clyde E. Martin, 1948). Based on thousands of carefully controlled in-depth interviews, the report concluded that 10 percent of all men are exclusively homosexual or nearly so, judged by both psychic stimulation and actual practice, for significant portions of their adult lives.

Moreover, the Kinsey study found that in the teenage years, between ages 15 and 20, between 23 and 24 percent of all men show "definite homosexual responses." This includes both those who are exclusively homosexual and those who mix more than incidental homosexual interest and activity with varying amounts of heterosexual interest and activity. (Between 15 and 18 per cent are at least as much homosexual as they are heterosexual [the midpoint of Kinsey's scale or higher].)

Thus, at least one in every ten teenage boys is exclusively or predominately homosexual; one in six has at least as much homosexual desire or activity or both as heterosexual desire or activity, and one in five has some homosexual component that is more than incidental. Reliable statistics for women are lacking, but "the best estimate is that homosexuality is found at least as frequently among women as among men," according to Jack H. Hedblom in *The Female Homosexual: Social and Attitudinal Dimensions* (1972).

If we assume that runaways are exclusively or predominately homosexual in the same proportions as the general population, then it is easy to see that a significant share of runaways are gay, exclusively or otherwise. But there is a good possibility that there might actually be a higher proportion of gays among runaways than among the general population of young people. Morris Kight, a founder of the Gay Community Services Center in Los Angeles, suggests that because of the special pressures felt by gay young people, especially in families and communities where homosexuality is sternly denounced, they are more likely to run away than are their heterosexual peers.

So much for statistics for the moment. Now a word about definitions. Throughout this chapter, we will use the words "gay" and "homosexual" as if they referred to a uniform, clearly identifiable set of people. This is a necessary shorthand, but we must ask the reader to bear in mind that it is deceptive.

As we have seen, there are varying degrees of homosexuality. The Kinsey study suggested that these could be described as a continuum, with seven divisions. On one end were those people who are exclusively heterosexual, and have had no homosexual fantasies and no homosexual activity. These, the study reported, constitute no more than half the male population. On the other end were those who are exclusively homosexual for at least three years during their adult lives. These constitute about 8 percent of the population. Then there are all those in between, including those who are almost exclusively homosexual and who, combined with the exclusively homosexual, help make up the 10 percent figure mentioned earlier.

Some of the anxiety attached to homosexuality in teenage years arises in young people who become aware of a certain amount of attraction in themselves to people of their own sex, and get terribly upset that they are "queer." Instead of looking at the matter as a dichotomy, and choosing one "side" or another, they would be better off taking a look at Kinsey's continuum and finding the spot that best describes their own balance.

In this chapter, we will address ourselves primarily to those who are exclusively or almost exclusively homosexual, but much of what we will say applied as well to those with different mixes. In fact, some things may apply more strongly to them, especially those who are not yet entirely sure where they fall.

Just as there are varying degrees of actual homosexual feelings and activities, there are also varying lifestyles and patterns of behavior among people who share those feelings and activities. You can't tell a book by its cover, and you can't tell a gay just by glitter. Some gays lean toward sequins and feathers; others stick to blue jeans and tee shirts. If you think you can tell who is gay and who is not just by appearance, forget it. Even gays themselves often have a hard time trying.

PARENTS

By far the most frequent reason gay runaways give for their decision to run is hassles with parents. In this, gay runaways may not be different from non-gay runaways, but the underlying tensions are probably deeper and more difficult to deal with.

Although different people discover their homosexual feelings and begin to act on them at widely different ages, there are many people in their teenage years who are already fully aware of their homosexual feelings. For them, the central problem is how to find a way to act on those feelings without blowing up their relationships with their parents.

The exact nature of the young person's situation depends on a number of variables. Different people face somewhat different problems depending on how the variables combine in their particular situations. These variables are:

1. Whether or not the young person's relationship with his or her parents in general is strong, honest and affectionate;

2. Whether one or both or neither of the parents know that the young person is gay, and whether the young person is aware of their knowledge or lack of knowledge;

3. The attitudes of each parent toward homosexuality, and the young person's awareness of their attitudes;
4. The amount of restriction the parents attempt to impose on the young person's ability to be out of the home after school and enjoy social and sexual activity;
5. The extent to which the parents attempt to pry into the young person's activity and affairs outside the home;
6. The extent to which the young person accepts homosexuality as his or her preferred style of sexual activity and has support from other people who accept it as a valid style, or conversely, the extent to which he or she has guilt feelings about being homosexual and feels alone and isolated; and
7. The young person's age and degree of independence from his or her parents.

Here are three illustrations of some of the ways these variables can combine:

Tommy

Tommy grew up in a middle-class black family. His father, a former Air Force officer, was confined to a hospital with an ailment similar to muscular dystrophy; Tommy lived with his mother and two younger brothers.

Tommy became aware of homosexual feelings at about age 13, when he was in junior high school. For three or four years, however, he bottled up those feelings, never talking about them with anyone and never acting on them except to "fool around" a little with other boys. Through the first two years of high school, he tried, with a certain amount of success, to pass for straight. When he succeeded in obtaining a transfer to a small, experimental school with a more liberal and open atmosphere than the previous school, he began to feel more able to open up about his gayness. He developed relationships with some men, and developed positive feelings about being gay.

He still did not get around to telling his mother, however, until one night he got into an argument with her. She told him she knew all about his gay friends and his "hangups." "It was like she had this secret that she could throw in my face, like I didn't know that she knew it," he said.

He said he was aware that she knew about his gayness, because she would frequently intercept calls and letters from gay friends. He felt unable to discuss it with her, however, and also felt unable to maintain contact with gay friends while living at home.

"The reason I left home was that I really felt I had to live two lives there," he said. "I had two younger brothers, and I had to make sure I didn't do anything gay around them. My mother didn't want me to bring any of my gay friends home. I wanted a place where my lover could come home and be with me. The only place we could see each other was at his place."

Paradoxically, the initial reaction of Tommy's mother when he did tell her he was gay was to tell him not to worry, it was "just a passing phase." "When I insisted I really was gay and that I wasn't worried about it, she said it was all this gay liberation stuff, getting young boys mixed up," Tommy said. In short, his mother had her suspicions all along, but did not want to admit that Tommy was really gay. When she finally had to admit it, she wanted to try to keep it covered up, apparently fearing he would somehow "infect" his younger brothers.

Tommy's mother has since apparently reconciled herself to his situation, and after a period of living with his lover he has moved back to live with his mother, while still seeing his lover regularly.

Van

Van grew up in a large, basically middle-class black family. His mother had divorced his father and remarried, and Van lived through his early teenage years with his mother and stepfather, plus his mother's six other children and his stepfather's four children from a previous marriage.

Van felt close to his mother, whom he says is "very understanding, and wants me to come back home." His relations with his brothers and sisters were apparently not overly close; most were older than him and had moved out of the home by the time he became a teenager. He attended a Catholic parochial school, where several of his close friends were also gay. His main reason for wanting to run away was his stepfather, a middle-grade blue-collar employee at a federal agency. Van had realized he was gay by age 12 and, even though he participated in track and other sports in high school, he felt his stepfather looked down on him for being gay. "He had nothing kind to say to me," Van said of his stepfather. "Everything that came out of his mouth was, 'Do this' or 'Do that.'" He felt that in many cases he was being unfairly singled out for harsh treatment. Van left home after one incident in which his stepfather woke him up at 4:30 one morning and ordered him to clean up after his mother's two pet poodles, who had soiled the bathroom floor. Van decided he had had enough of such authoritarianism and left. He spent some time at a runaway house in the city, and has since been living with friends. He is now 19, and was 16 when he ran away. For the most part, has held jobs that, although low skilled, were sufficient to provide him a living. He has little or no contact with his family now.

Rich

Rich grew up in a large, old former farm house on a sizeable tract of land, no longer farmed, in a suburban area. His mother, a businesswoman who owned apartment buildings and small businesses in the area, had divorced his father, an engineer. The father moved to another state while the mother raised Rich, an older sister and a younger brother.

Rich had his first homosexual experience in his early teens. Because his mother was away from the house often, he was able to visit friends and often had them over to his house, so he did not lack a social and sexual life.

Although his mother did not keep a constant surveillance of his activities, on the occasions when she did catch him staying out too late or otherwise committing some infraction, she reacted strongly. On one of these occasions, she sent Rich and his younger brother to stay with her ex-husband, in the hope that he could control Rich better. Instead, Rich expanded his activity, bringing sexual partners over to his father's house on a regular basis. When the father found out, he sent Rich to stay with an aunt and uncle who had cared for him for a time several years earlier when his mother was ill.

There, Rich lived with unaccustomed restrictions on his activity. He managed to find ways to evade these restrictions somewhat, but for the most part he began to concentrate for the first time on school work, and as a result his grades soared.

Eventually, however, the relationship with his aunt and uncle soured. His aunt constantly tried to convince him that he should see a psychiatrist for his homosexuality, a suggestion he firmly rejected and resented. Even more strongly resented were invasions of his privacy, when his aunt or uncle would open letters from friends with whom he had had relationships while living with his father. Rich began to feel that his aunt and uncle were "trying to plan my life for me."

The break came when his aunt and uncle insisted on accompanying him backstage to a school play in which he was a production assistant, on the grounds that a bottle of gin was missing from their liquor cabinet and they feared Rich and his friends would consume it all during a planned cast party. (In fact, they had long since consumed it all.) In a flash of anger and resentment, Rich literally ran away, bolting suddenly for a patch of woods while his aunt and uncle were on the way to the car to take him to the play.

He hitchhiked back to the area where his mother lived, going first to a friend's house. He phoned his mother, and she drove out immediately for a tearful reunion. He lived with her peacefully for several months, but eventually he began to take part in gay activity, including a trip to New York City for a gay pride march. She told Rich she wanted him never to do anything like that again. "These are sick people," she told him. "They need psychiatric help." She displayed a very anti-gay attitude, in Rich's view, and soon he decided he wanted to live with gay people rather than at home.

The final break came when his mother discovered that he had been growing marijuana plants in a secret attic compartment of the house. She told his brother and sister that she was going to have the police arrest Rich as soon as he came home, so when he came up the driveway a few hours later they ran to warn him. He quickly gathered some belongings, kissed his brother goodbye, and left to stay with some friends. With some help from a counselor at a runaway house, he soon found a job and a permanent place to stay, and is now active in a gay youth organization. He says he still has strong feelings of real love for his mother, but is happy not to live with her any more, and is now concerned for the health of his younger brother, who is living in his mother's house, largely unsupervised. Rich is now 18 and on his own.

These cases illustrate common reactions of many parents of gay young people. In many cases, probably the majority, the parents perceive their child's homosexuality as a sickness which, like cancer in years past, is something to hide from the neighbors. This is closely related to the "where did we go wrong?" reaction. Most parents know little about homosexuality except what they pick up from the media, which, at least until recently, has largely reflected the negative attitudes that have in the past pervaded the psychiatric profession. In Spring of 1974, 58 percent of the psychiatrists voting in a referendum among members of the American Psychiatric Association voted to uphold an earlier decision of the Association's board of trustees eliminating homosexuality, as such, from the organization's official list of mental disorders. But it will take some time for this change in official psychiatric definition to filter down to the general public.

Parents who feel somehow to blame for their child's homosexuality would damage only their own self-esteem if they went no further than that. But many parents are not content to leave it at that, and instead attempt to impose their own guilt feelings on their gay children. They attempt to have the child "cured" by visits to a psychiatrist or other professional. Meanwhile, they attempt to restrict the activity of their child, preventing him or her from enjoying the kind of social life that a heterosexual teenage usually takes for granted. In some cases, one of the underlying motives is simply to make sure that "the neighbors don't find out," on the assumption that the discovery of a homosexual child would bring shame on the family.

This pattern of reaction can be seen in both Tommy's mother

and Rich's mother. Both viewed their sons' homosexuality as something either to be cured or sent out of sight. The case of Van's stepfather was different, probably because the stepfather felt no guilt for the way Van turned out, and so was freer in expressing open hostility. Although this case involved a step-parent, similar open hostility is occasionally expressed by natural parents toward their gay offspring. As we have seen, both patterns of parental reaction—feelings of shame and feelings of hostility— can lead young people to run away.

Contrast these patterns with the response of a mother who had close relations with her son before she found he was homosexual, and has, if anything, strengthened those relations since.

When her son, who was then a senior in high schol, came to her in a distraught, penitent mood and told her he was a homosexual, she told him, "Well, honey, it's not the end of the world." But, she says now, "inside, I thought it *was* the end of the world, because I didn't really know much about homosexuality. I really hadn't had much contact with it, and I had a lot of the stereotyped ideas about it."

"I was surprised, because I didn't want him to be that way. I thought, maybe it's just a phase. I did all the rationalization in my mind."

She said that she realized her son had been distraught because of the secrecy he had tried to keep, and said she felt "pleased that he could tell me this, even though I didn't want to know it at the time."

She went through many of the same feelings most other parents of gays experience, including wondering what had gone "wrong" and worrying about where her son was and what he was doing when he went out of the house. But she still kept herself open to him. She discussed the subject with him several times, and read several books to increase her knowledge of homosexuality. Finally, when she saw the heartbreak and depression he experienced after he broke up with a lover, she realized that gay relationships do involve real love and affection, and not just homosexual sex acts. By staying open to her son, she has been able to see him as a full person and not just an extension of herself. This is probably the main thing that makes her different from the parents we have discussed earlier.

This parent has now organized a "Parents of Gays" group in an effort to help other parents think through their reactions. Such groups have been formed in a handful of large cities, and could be helpful to thousands of parents if formed more widely. They will be discussed in more detail in a later section.

The parents who have not yet reached the point that this mother has—the parents who are not open with their children, who view their children's homosexuality as sick and shameful, and who attempt to impose unusual restrictions on their gay children—are the parents whose gay children are most likely to run away, given the opportunity and necessity.

Sometimes, a young person will have enough self-confidence to successfully "wear down" his or her parents, and win a measure of freedom from restrictions by simply making it so hard for the parents to impose them that they give up the effort. This can result in a tenuous *modus vivendi* which lasts until the child goes to college or otherwise leaves the home.

In other situations, a young person will rely on friends at school or elsewhere in the community for emotional support, and will be able to survive a period of parental restrictions, while waiting anxiously for the day when he or she can move out of the house.

In other situations, however, running away can be the most reasonable alternative. This is especially true in situations where parents' attitudes are especially hostile; where parents insist on unwanted "therapy," which occasionally even involves shock treatment or aversion therapy; where restrictions on social life or invasions of privacy become too odious, or where other ways of coping while remaining at home are not available.

Counselors who have advised gay runaways note that in many cases the gay young person returns home after a period and finds a much better atmosphere. "Parents realize, often for the first time, that their youngster is a force, that they have here another person, and they have got to deal with him on his own terms," commented Frank Kameny of the Mattachine Society of Washington, a long-time gay activist who receives many calls from gay young people seeking advice. Short of changing a parents' attitude toward homosexuality, the realization that their child has his or her own will and personality can "help them at least tolerate something they can't swallow completely," Kameny said.

Some runaway counseling organizations have developed methods of contacting parents and trying to bring about reconciliations when possible. A description of such a program in a runaway house especially for gays will appear in a later section.

For a particularly valuable discussion of the problems encountered when a gay young person decides it is time to tell his or her parents, read *Society and the Healthy Homosexual,* by Dr. George Weinberg, available in paperback from Anchor/Doubleday.

PEERS

Next to parents, the problems gay young people face most often revolve around peers. This may take one of two forms: actual harassment of one sort or another, or fear of such harassment and consequent efforts to avoid it.

Anyone who has survived adolescence can remember that "faggot," "queer," "homo," "sissy," and "punk" are among the most frequently used derogatory terms in the vocabulary of people that age. At this period, young people are learning how to mold their behavior to fit the images of "what men are like" and "what women are like," as they pick up such images from parents, television, books, other adults and each other. People whose behavior doesn't quite fit these images are scorned and derided—probably as a result of the well-known psychological mechanism of heaping scorn on someone with certain characteristics to reassure yourself that you don't share them.

Tommy's experience is an example of how this pressure can work. He recalls that in high school one of his classmates acted somewhat effeminately, and was consequently the butt of jokes, jeers and pranks. When mocking jokes about homosexuality were told, this boy's name was used in them, sometimes as the basis for puns. At the time, Tommy had not yet come to terms with his own homosexuality, and shared in heaping scorn upon this boy. "People who were effeminate really disgusted me then," he recalls.

During this time, Tommy himself began to struggle with his homosexual feelings. At first, like many young people do when they first become aware of such feelings, he tried to hide them. "I would stand around with the other boys and stare right along with them whenever a girl walked by; but all the time I was wanting to get it on with the guys." He developed many mannerisms that were not instinctual to him, such as "making sure I crossed my legs with one ankle on the other knee, and not with both ankles together, like girls do."

He managed to pass for straight like this for several years, at the cost of a great deal of psychic energy. Finally, to his relief, he developed some gay friends with whom he could be open, and at about the same time transferred to a smaller school that had a more tolerant atmosphere, in which he felt less threatened.

Larry, a member of a gay collective in Columbia, Maryland, tells of a similar experience:

"When I was young I thought other boys were too rough. I liked to draw and paint and I avoided any kind of sports for fear of being laughed at. I was ridiculed and called a sissy. Adults, teachers and my peers made me feel I just wasn't making it as a boy. My mother was always trying to get me to play baseball 'like the other boys.' I really felt like an outcast."

"I had a classmate, Hank, who tormented me for months. He beat me up every day and called me a fairy so everyone could laugh. I ran between classes, missed the bus, stayed home sick, spent hours worrying and did everything possible to avoid being publicly humiliated and beaten. But I kept my fear to myself. I spent hours crying alone and thinking about a revenge. I fantasized about being strong and beating up Hank."

Finally, Larry had his revenge. He passed through a bout with a kidney disease by diligently exercising his body to make it stronger. "I was driven intensely by my fear of being ridiculed and beaten and my anger at those who wouldn't accept me for what I was." He finally got on the high school football team, became co-captain of the wrestling team . . . and beat up Hank. More recently, he has rejected the kind of competitive role that he felt forced into at that time.

It is unclear whether the kind of harassment that Tommy

helped inflict on his classmate, and that Larry himself suffered, is by itself a motivation for many young gay people to run away. It is likely, however, that such harassment, or the inability to deal with homosexual feelings because of the fear of such harassment, can contribute to the anxiety and the confusion which some young runaways feel about their situations.

Morris Kight of Los Angeles reports that many of the gay young people who flee to the Gay Community Services Center there are the more "effeminized" or "the rebels who refuse to act straight." There are signs that an increasing number of gay young people, at least in more sophisticated urban and surburban areas, are becoming "rebels." Not all of them wind up being forced to flee, either. There are some who entirely self-confident, display gay liberation buttons, and make no effort to hide their feelings. In some cases, they gain the respect of peers and others with their courage and honesty and are free of harassment.

One critical factor that seems to make the difference between whether a gay young person will be able to withstand pressure from straight peers is whether he or she is in touch with other gay people. In some schools, gay students who have managed to "find" each other form informal cliques and friendship patterns. These not only provide emotional support, but sometimes are useful in helping deter harassment from straight students. "If there is any indication that gays are getting together, it will tone down the harassment, just because of the simple knowledge on the part of other students that you're not dealing with only one person," according to Frank Kameny of Washington.

A number of cities have "gay youth" organizations in which gay young people from a number of schools get together. Their activities generally include informal "rap sessions," which are useful for trading experiences and building a sense in each individual that he or she is not alone and is not unique.

It is also helpful for gay students to know that there is at least one teacher or counselor at their school with whom they can talk honestly and openly without fear of rejection or condescension. Kameny says that occasionally high school counselors ask him how they can identify gay students and offer to help them. He replies that it is a simple matter: "You know what the channels of communication are in your school, whether formal or informal. See to it that word gets spread around to students who are homosexual that they can come to you and be handled nonjudgementally. They'll come in droves."

SELF-IMAGE

Many aspects of gay young peoples' problems with parents and peers touch on a third problem area which merits a brief separate discussion. That is the problem of self-image.

As has been seen, gay young people have few sources for a positive image of homosexuality. Many are raised by parents who are as ignorant of the subject as they are hostile, or who at best view it as a "temporary aberration" or "sickness" that with time and perhaps some expensive doctors' bills can be cured. They grow up with peers who pick up the prevailing homophobic attitude and express it in painful, cutting mockery or sometimes more violent ways. They are exposed to mass media which typically ignore the existence of homosexuality, or treat it as a subject for off-color jokes or stereotypical cardboard characterizations in TV and movie plots. They learn quickly that homosexual behavior is viewed as sinful by some, sick by most others, and illegal by most legislatures and courts.

Arguments regarding these attitudes toward homosexuality have been waged in many places, and will not be repeated here. Several of the books listed in the resources section at the end of this chapter contain illuminating discussions on the subject.

It is the consequences for the gay young person's view of himself or herself with which we are concerned. These consequences are frequently severe, and sometimes literally fatal.

One of the most common experiences of gay people is the experience of severe depression and suicidal thoughts during the period when they become aware that their sexual fantasies and desires are directed toward people of their own sex, but are not yet ready to identify themselves as "homosexual," and are, in many cases, not yet ready to act on those desires.

For many gay people, this period of "coming out" is a time of great anxiety and depression because they are painfully confronting the fact that their sexual identity, one of the most basic aspects of their identity as a person, is something that has in their experience always been regarded as unspeakable and unclean. They apply this to their entire identity, and begin to feel akin to the lowest form of life. Most crucially, they feel no one will care for them because of this aspect of their personality, which they try to keep hidden for that reason. Often, they know no one else like themselves, and therefore feel unique, alone and helpless. Unless they are given hope that they are not alone, and that someone does care, they turn to thoughts of ending it all. A few make attempts; some succeed.

For most, a way out of the slough of despondency is offered by a friend with whom they feel close enough to share their secret. In their minds, this is often built up as a major crisis: will my friend reject me? Fortunately, in many instances the crisis passes: the friend does not immediately run from the room and break off all relations. A step toward a positive self-image has been taken. Another close friend, another step. Soon, with enough support, the gay person is willing to tell about his feelings to anybody who'll listen—eventually even parents or counselors.

In recent years, as the gay liberation movement has spread, many young gay people have had the opportunity to publicly proclaim that they are "gay and proud." While this proclamation of essentially private preference may seem odd or even distasteful to some, it can be understood as a way of eradicating the memory of those months or years when this important part of the person's identity was kept hidden—"in the closet," as the phrase goes in gay argot.

Like the problem of harassment from peers, the problem of negative self-image may not by itself be a cause for running away in most cases, but seems likely to intensify whatever discontents already exist with the young person's situation.

In some cases, the act of running away does not by itself clear away feelings of self-doubt and depression. It may result in a better, more supportive environment for the young person to deal with them, but this process may take a long time. The experience of Jack is an example of this.

Jack grew up in a family environment that put strong pressures on him to conform to their narrow image of what he should be—a successful student who made good grades and would enter a good college and a profession. Although he is in fact intelligent, he was highly sensitive to ways in which he failed to completely fit his parents' design; one was his homosexual feelings. When these became apparent, he felt isolated and alone, with no friends to support him.

It was in this frame of mind that he ran away. With the help of a runaway house, he was placed in a residential boarding school. Tuition was paid by his parents, who were contacted by the runaway house and were relieved to find that he was getting assistance of that sort. He dropped out of the boarding school after a few months, however, because he found no support for his need to explore his homosexuality and other differences from other people.

He then moved into a group foster home operated by the runaway house. This was a place where young people could stay for a period of up to a few months while they worked through their plans for what to do in the longer run. Even there, he apparently felt a need for more direction and guidance than the staff felt willing to give. He sought counseling from a gay men's counseling organization, and over a period of time developed a heavily dependent relationship with his counselor. His counselor describes Jack as unable to form close relationships easily, unsure of himself, and unable to take much initiative. Despite this, Jack has managed to support himself and function independently, holding down a job and paying his own rent. With the kind of supportive relationship he needs, he might develop a more positive image of himself.

COUNSELING APPROACHES

It is clear that the young person who is predominately homosexual encounters special problems that the predominately heterosexual young person does not. It should not be surprising that the gay young person also needs a special approach. The following suggestions are drawn from comments made by gay runaways, gay counselors who have assisted many gay runaways, and straight counselors who have successfully developed rapport with several gay runaways.

The beginning of wisdom is to admit your ignorance. This aphorism applies also to beginning efforts by straight counselors to assist gay young people in thinking through their situation and charting a course after running away from home.

Probably the most common mistake made by such counselors, a mistake which is likely to destroy most chance of establishing a constructive relationship with a gay young person, is to assure the young person that they "understand his problem" and sympathize with him, then suggest that maybe he would be better off if he went to a psychiatrist for help. Young gay people term this the "phony liberal" approach.

Tommy, the black gay runaway whom we met earlier, compared this approach to that of some whites during the 1960's who assured blacks that they tolerated them. "These were people who said, 'I don't care about color; it's all the same to me. We're all brothers—even though my folks came from England and your folks came from darkest Africa,' " Tommy mimicked.

The problem he was identifying is that of papering over unconscious feelings of uneasiness about the subject of homosexuality with hearty assurances of tolerance. The problem arises because, just as many whites unconsciously develop racist attitudes despite an intellectual commitment to equality, so many heterosexuals who have had little contact with homosexuals harbor inaccurate and derogatory stereotypes of homosexuals in their minds, despite a theoretical acknowledgment that gays should be accorded equal rights.

"If I were a straight counselor and I had to counsel a gay guy," Tommy commented, "I would feel comfortable talking about things that didn't have to do with gayness. But if I didn't know much about gay people, I would want to meet up with other gay people before I tried to deal with his gayness."

Two straight counselors who have had success in dealing with gay runaways agree that making contacts with gay people and getting to know them as people who are gay is a good way to prepare yourself for counseling gay young people.

These counselors, Mary Trevor and Lynn Rosenfield of Runaway House in Washington, D. C., said that one of the first gay runaways they counseled was a particular challenge because of his "flamboyance." This young man, named Jerry, had at first been placed in a group home run by the county government of a heavily working-class surburban county. There he was "ridiculed and hassled" by the other young people because "they felt there was something different about him. They didn't necessarily know he was gay, but he carried a purse and looked like a hippy."

At that house, Jerry generally "did what he was supposed to do, but the other kids made him a scapegoat," Lynn and Mary reported. They said the staff at that house, whom they came in contact with after Jerry ran from that house to Runaway House, "didn't support him until it was too late. They didn't call the other kids down when they were hassling Jerry; they didn't stick up for Jerry in front of the other kids." The staff at that suburban group home later acknowledged their error.

A large part of the reason for the suburban counselors' failure to help Jerry, Lynn and Mary said, was apparently their failure to confront their own feelings about homosexuality. By contrast, Lynn and Mary described their own efforts to examine their own attitudes on the issue when Jerry confronted them with it.

"Mary and I talked at the beginning about what it was like for us to be working with Jerry," Lynn said. "We were not really feeling that we knew much about gayness. We didn't have the gut-level experience of dealing with a kid who was so up front about it."

"Jerry was always challenging you to confront those issues," Mary commented.

"He was challenging you to reject him because he was gay," Lynn added. "That's what had always happened to him in the past."

"He didn't understand why we didn't, too," Mary remarked. She explained the thinking she had to go through as a result of Jerry's challenge: "What Jerry confronted in me was my feelings around gayness in other people, in myself, in people I relate to day-to-day. I face it in all our kids—we have some redneck kids here and I have to face their prejudices every day.

"A gay young person confronts in me my feelings about sexuality. To the degree that I have worked those things out, that's the degree that I can relate to him or her honestly and effectively.... We say to ourselves that we're open to anything, at least on an intellectual level. When we're confronted with it, we have to bring it down to a gut level and ask ourselves, 'OK, am I really open to gays?' "

Both Lynn and Mary acknowledged that they were not ready for some of Jerry's more flamboyant moments, such as his occasional practice of putting on a woman's wig and dress and loudly drawing attention to himself. But they tried to honestly express their feelings. Rather than pretending to ignore him, they told him that his behavior made them uncomfortable and that they weren't used to it. This was said, however, simply as honest reporting of their reactions, not as a command to him to stop his behavior.

"My philosophy is to not deny my own feelings, biases and experiences, but at the same time to be open to where the young person is," Mary said. She and Lynn prefer this approach to that of the "well-meaning liberal" who might tell a gay young person, " 'If that's what you want, it's cool with me,' and then if something comes along that really freaks them out, not be honest about their reactions and take it out on the kid in some other way."

Persons connected with counseling groups who want to design programs to meet the special needs of gay young people should examine the model of the Gay Community Services Center in Los Angeles. Its services to runaways are tied into a variety of other services offered to all segments of the gay community. This sort of integrated program has great value. Among the segments that relate directly to runaways are:

1. A residential house and informal connections with other communal houses that can provide a supportive living situation for the runaway. This not only helps take care of an essential need for housing, but can also help the young

person think through his or her situation in a nonthreat-
ening atmosphere, among fellow gays.

2. A youth group. As described earlier, this is a "rap" group,
   meeting weekly and open to all. Trained "facilitators" participate in order to help the meeting proceed, but are careful not to steer the direction themselves. In addition,
   members of the group act as peer counselors for young people who show up at the center seeking help. This sometimes
   involves accompanying the young person to a VD clinic, or
   to a school to register, or other places where there is a need
   for moral support and a little hand-holding.

3. Family counseling. Staff and volunteer counselors, including several mental health professionals, are able to bring
   together runaways with their families in many cases, as
   needed. The counselors try to facilitate an open discussion
   of each family member's feelings, to encourage communication that often was lacking before. Sometimes these sessions
   result in emotional reunions; other times the family remains
   apart. The center arranges such sessions only after some
   degree of trust has been established between the counselor
   and the young person, and only if the young person wants
   such a session. Some young people participate in group discussion sessions to help them think through their sexual
   identity and other concerns before they confront their parents in these sessions.

Whenever possible, the center tries to bring the young person
together not only with parents but also with others who have
significant influences on his or her life. This may include the
family minister, brothers and sisters, possibly a doctor. The idea is
that all the people who have a role in some aspect of the young
person's life should be aware of his or her feelings and those of
the other important people in his life.

RESOURCES

The following are individuals and organizations who have been
helpful in preparing this chapter. This list does not pretend to

cover all those groups who could be of great help to counselors dealing with gay young people, but these organizations can sometimes make referrals. See *Gayellow Pages,* listed below, for references to gay organizations in many cities.

Gay Community Services Center, 1614 Wilshire Blvd., Los Angeles, Calif. 90017. Phone (213) 482-3062. Morris Kight, founder; Don Kilhefner and Betty Taylor, Executive Directors.

Mattachine Society of Washington, D. C., 5020 Cathedral Avenue, N.W., Washington, D. C. 20013. Phone (202) 363-3881. Frank Kameny, President.

National Gay Task Force, 80 Fifth Avenue, New York, N.Y. Phone 212-741-1010. Nathalie Rockhill, Coordination Director; Thomas H. Smith, Community Services Director.

Special Approaches in Juvenile Assistance (Runaway House), 1743—18th Street, N.W., Washington, D. C. 20009. Phone (202) 234-4383. Lynn Rosenfield or Mary Trevor, staff.

REFERENCES

Following are selected books for those who desire a better understanding of gay people. For a more complete listing of works on the subject, consult *A Gay Bibliography,* Third Revision, January 1974, published by the Task Force on Gay Liberation of the American Library Association. It is available from Barbara Gittings, Box 2383, Philadelphia, Pennsylvania 19103.

Altman, Dennis: *Homosexuality: Oppression and Liberation.* Hardback, Dutton; paperback, Avon, 1974.

Clark, Lige, and Nichols, Jack: *I Have More Fun With You Than Anybody.* St. Martin's, 1972.

Fisher, Peter: *The Gay Mystique.* Stein and Day, 1972.

Hoffman, Martin: *The Gay World.* Hardback, Basic Books; paperback, Bantam, 1968.

Martin, Del, and Lyon, Phyllis: *Lesbian/Woman.* Hardback, Glide Publications; paperback, Bantam, 1972.

Weinberg, George: *Society and the Healthy Homosexual.* Hardback, St. Martin's; paperback, Anchor/Doubleday, 1972.

Weinberg, Martin S.. and Williams, Colin J.: *Male Homosexuals: their problems and adaptations.* Oxford University Press (hardback only), 1974.

Weltge, Ralph W. (ed.): *The Same Sex: an appraisal of homosexuality.* Pilgrim/United Church Press (paperback), 1969.

Among the many periodicals listed in the Gay Bibliography, these are likely to be of most direct interest to counselors:

Homosexual Counseling Journal. Journal for mental health and behavioral sciences professions. Haworth Press, 53 W. 72 Street, New York, New York 10023. Quarterly. $12/yr. individual; $25/year library rate.

The Advocate. Nationally distributed newspaper, covering gay news from around the country. 2121 S. ElCamino Real, Suite 307, San Mateo, California, 94403. $9/per year.

Gayellow Pages. Classified nationwide directory of gay organizations, including counseling centers, gay hotlines, activist organizations, gay youth groups, and other information sources. Issued three times a year. P.O. Box 292, Village Station, New York, N.Y. 10014. $5/issue.

SOME INDICES OF PREDICTION OF DELINQUENT BEHAVIOR

Henry Raymaker, Jr.

- EARLY DELINQUENT MANIFESTATIONS
- NEEDS FOR PSYCHOLOGICAL EVALUATION
- JUVENILE DELINQUENTS AND PROJECTIVE TECHNIQUES
- NEED TO BE SENSITIVE TO ORGANIC FACTORS
- SELF-CONCEPT AND THE JUVENILE DELINQUENT
- COMMUNITY RESPONSIBILITY

A T A TIME when crime rates are increasing, especially in offenses by young people, a review of signs of juvenile delinquency or indices of prediction, along with a review of the contribution that a practicing psychologist can make, is appropriate.

The detection of early signs of delinquency is most likely to occur in the home and school. The loss of interest in school subjects and conflicts with authority figures in the home and school often proceed some acting-out behavior which finally force society to respond and make an official case of juvenile delinquency. It is the sensitivity and motivation of the teachers to make referrals to guidance centers and professionals and the willingness of parents to seek help when these early signs are detected that could lead to a reduction and prevention of juvenile

67

delinquency. Also, parents who are sensitive to early manifestations of delinquent behavior can take corrective action.

EARLY DELINQUENT MANIFESTATIONS

Some of these early signs are resentment of authority figures in the home and school and overt conflicts, resentment of over-protection, resentment of limits and discipline, loss of interest in school subjects and obvious underachievements, confusion associated with inconsistent discipline, impulsiveness associated with permissiveness, suggestibility associated with peer group anti-social influences, frustration in the child and a need for compensatory behavior, compulsive stealing associated with poverty, involvement with drugs which usually has emotional and social motivations, etc.

There are many ways a child or adolescent may show tendencies toward delinquency. Also, in each case there are different origins, meaning and a matter of degree. The practicing psychologist, counselor, teacher, parent and society are faced with understanding multiple forms of delinquency and multiple causes that require an individual and clinical approach.

NEEDS FOR PSYCHOLOGICAL EVALUATION

To understand a youth and his behavior and formulate predictions a psychological evaluation of the intelligence, achievement, personality and feelings of the youth, along with a family and social history, is necessary. This provides the evidence to determine causes and early signs, needs, frustrations, infer predictions, and plan treatment or guidance.

The majority of young people who come to the attention of psychologists and court workers appear to have normal or average intelligence. Determining this dimension of the youth's profile can make our predictions and placement realistic and will maximize success. We do often see in this population underachievement in school subjects. Evidence that the youth is functioning below his native or potential level such as observing that his achievement scores are often below his I.Q. and grade placement can identify problems which when corrected may prevent delinquency. Many delinquents are functioning below their ability level and are behind in their achievement. One great need which exists in our school systems is to reach these children with remedial instruction and the possibility of these resources existing influences our predictive judgment.

In cases where the juvenile delinquent is mentally retarded and this is confirmed by individual intelligence testing, we can often reduce or control delinquency by removing a major source of frustration by placing the child in a special class within the school system for educable mentally retarded children. This reduces the stress and the feelings of rejection that the retarded child shows, which often is the frustration that causes his delinquency or aggression. The success and acceptance that the retarded child feels in a special class may meet the need that will modify the behavior pattern and increase conformity. Consistent discipline, structure and appropriate school placement appear to be the treatment needs of the delinquent who is mentally retarded and at the appropriate age referral to the vocational rehabilitation agency is needed. The degree that these resources exist in the community is relative to predicting the behavior of the child.

JUVENILE DELINQUENTS & PROJECTIVE TECHNIQUES

In the evaluation of the adolescent a sensitive instrument, which provides the psychologist with a sampling of the youth's feelings, attitudes and types of identifications, is the Thematic Apperception Test, or projective technique. The themes and stories which the youth creates on the picture cards in this technique provide meaningful insights into the youth's underlying identifications, feelings and often reveal long felt frustrated needs. Documentation in these areas may identify signs of the degree of the delinquency trend and needs in the youth's personality that are relevant to prediction and management. Experience shows that projecting hostility and aggression is often one of the most frequent themes that a delinquent develops in the stories he creates on this test.

A second frequent theme is the fact that many youths identify with human figures who are depressed and are moody, introspective, or resentful in areas of authority, restrictions, rejections, etc. A third frequent theme is the fact that many youths also project a need to be successful and identify with human figures who are striving for success and recognition. An observation that we frequently see in average or bright adolescents who are in custody because of their delinquency is an admission of faults and acts of delinquency and projecting desires to be a better and more successful person. They try to give the impression that they have learned their lesson and are going to try to do better.

Sometimes these adolescents show abilities at manipulating. Often, however, their comments suggest an awareness of guilt and a need for help. There are content areas where a majority of juvenile delinquents usually project feelings and attitudes on the Thematic Apperception Test and can be one of the most helpful clinical techniques that the practicing psychologist can utilize.

NEED TO BE SENSITIVE TO ORGANIC FACTORS

In the battery of tests used by the psychologist are also measurements that can identify organic brain dysfunctioning where in a small minority of these cases some subtle organic deficit may be partially responsible for aggressive or anti-social behavior. In addition to the tests of intelligence and personality, a sensitive instrument in detecting organicity is the Bender Gestalt test where the child has to copy on paper a series of geometric designs. It is important to rule out organic damage or factors and when identified referral to medical consultation and appropriate treatment and planning may control the aggressive behavior of the child. These awarenesses also help the teacher, counselor and parent to better understand and relate to the child. These determinations are relevant to predictive judgments on the course of the child's behavior and adjustment.

SELF-CONCEPT AND THE JUVENILE DELINQUENT

In predicting the behavior of the juvenile delinquent or estimating response to treatment it is useful for the practicing psychologist to determine the self-concept of the youth. The delinquent usually shows inadequate self-confidence or sees himself in negative ways or overcompensates for these feelings by being openly aggressive and hostile. The delinquent who maintains a negative self-image may continue to behave accordingly as a way of expressing hostility. It is the analyses of the origin of these perceptions and emotions that often are helpful in achieving self-awareness and insight and permit the delinquent, psychologist, counselor, and others to take steps to resolve and modify these behavior patterns.

The practicing psychologist may be able to infer the self-concept of the youth from the youth's identifications and projections on the Thematic Apperception Test. As a supplement to this, a practical approach to determining these self-perceptions is to ask the youth to write a letter about himself indicating how he sees himself, how he sees his problems and how he feels. Also, it is useful to have the youth complete a sentence completion test as many self-concept projections are revealed by this approach.

Therefore, the practicing psychologist's approach to the problem of juvenile delinquency and the study of prognostic signs is a responsibility to evaluate the intelligence and personality of the child or adolescent, determine his needs, attitudes, feelings, self-concept, review the social history, make recommendations, and be available as a treatment consultant.

It is in the focusing of the recommendations that a sensitivity to the indices of prediction is important as we strive to reduce delinquent behavior patterns. That is, the psychologist needs to make recommendations that may reduce the frustration in the child's life or meet the particular needs in each unique case that will remove the causes of delinquency. It is necessary that the community plan resources that can follow through on these recommendations, which usually include a progressive juvenile court, child guidance clinics, special education classes and consultation with the school system, social agencies such as rehabilitation services, and professional personnel working together in effective communication and coordination.

A psychological evaluation in isolation of the child's environment and continuing influences and resources is an academic exercise. When needs are documented and resources in the community are lacking, then it is the success which we achieve in getting community and social action to develop these resources that will make each community a low predictive or a high predictive environment for success in reducing juvenile delinquency.

In order to formulate or identify signs or indicators which may be used to infer predictions the clinical case method does reveal a pattern or similarities which suggest areas that are relevant in the etiology, treatment, prognoses and prevention of juvenile delinquency. The inferences from this practical experience can offer some indices of prediction. Also, possible warning or early signs in the general pre-school and elementary school age population can assist us when parents, teachers and society respond and try correcting problems or meeting frustrated needs before delinquent behavior is manifested or comes to the attention of the court.

COMMUNITY RESPONSIBILITY

It is through a mental hygiene and public health principle of prevention that the magnitude of the juvenile delinquency problem in society must eventually be approached. Juvenile court judges are becoming more aware of the significance of meeting needs, arranging for individual and family counseling and treating the emotional dynamics of delinquency. In this corrective and rehabilitative process the involvement of family, school and supportive service agencies working together can increase the prospect of success as more people see the need for treating causes, frustrations and emotions in contrast to simple removal or isolation of the delinquent from society. It is in the area of social change such as the removal of double standards or the inconsistencies in society that additional progress can be made as often many causes and signs of delinquency are related to poor examples of adults.

A community which is dynamic and progressive can cope with problems of juveniles and create a more favorable environment. The worker in this field needs to be involved in social change as behavior is a function of internal and external motivation and influences.

In summary, juvenile delinquency can be reduced by a community sensitive to early signs and indices of prediction of delinquency and can take corrective action. Also, the child who becomes involved in juvenile court action can be evaluated and helped to become a more satisfied and productive person as the sources of his frustrations are removed by planning and counseling.

A forthright approach is for the community to recognize its problems and try to communicate and offer services for this important group of young people, correct its own shortcomings by removing inconsistencies or double standards, provide healthy identifications for youth and provide adequate education, recreation and guidance facilities.

GUIDED GROUP INTERACTION: A REHABILITATIVE APPROACH

JAMES O. FINCKENAUER

- ■ AN EVALUATION OF THE IMPACT OF GUIDED GROUP INTERACTION
- ■ GROUP SIX—A CASE STUDY
- ■ ASSESSMENT OF GROUP SIX
- ■ EPILOGUE OF GROUP SIX

THE RESIDENTIAL GROUP CENTERS in New Jersey have represented a unique project in using a group approach in the treatment of juvenile delinquency. Histories of the evolution of the "Highfields" program, including descriptions and careful evaluations, have been presented elsewhere and need not be replicated here. However, the core of the program, the guided group interaction sessions which represent the key to success in any effort to duplicate the Highfields concept, need to be re-examined in greater detail for the benefit of those practitioners attempting to implement guided group interaction. Such implementation is now beginning or ongoing in juvenile correctional institutions, residential and nonresidential community-based rehabilitation facilities, junior high and high schools, police department juvenile aid

74

bureaus, etc; and it is being used with committed adolescent offenders, parolees, school dropouts, boys, girls, school problem
children, probationers and unemployed youths.

Guided group interaction has been defined as the use of "free
discussion in a friendly supportive atmosphere to reeducate delinquents to accept the restrictions of society by finding greater
personal satisfaction in conforming to social rules than in following delinquent patterns." It attempts to aid group members by
developing understanding of their current problems through
interaction with others. The subjects discussed in the guided
group revolve around current problems of group members and
of the group itself. These problems emerge as a result of interaction with significant others, primarily peers, and in the group
meetings themselves are crucial to guided group interaction.

The guided group sessions serve as a means for stabilizing
the lives of adolescents, and as a medium through which each
young person is able to come to grips with his or her problems.
The major emphasis in this technique is on the group and its
development, rather than upon an exhaustive analysis of each
group member. Thus, the method is only somewhat similar to
group therapy. Unlike formal group therapy, the group leader
need not be a clinician. More important than any formal academic
training are a perceptive understanding of adolescents and their
problems, particularly the influence of peer pressures upon behavior; an empathic ability to establish rapport with the members
of the particular group without being threatening or threatened;
and an understanding of the group process in changing human
behavior.

Guided group interaction is considered to be most effective
with adolescents because they are perhaps more responsive to peer
influences than any other particular age group. Because participation in the group process requires an intellectual understanding
of the complexities and subtleties of that process, it is not desirable
to include as group participants any young people who are mentally retarded to an extent that would not permit them to function intellectually in the program.

Persons with severe psychological disorders (advanced neuroses or psychoses) also should be excluded for several important reasons:

1. The group pressures can be extremely threatening and damaging to an individual psychologically incapable of handling them.
2. The group leader in all likelihood does not possess the necessary psychological or psychiatric training to deal with severe mental or emotional disorders.
3. The group members who are the most important change agents will neither understand nor be able to cope with mentally or emotionally disordered individuals.

Eight to twelve members is considered to be the optimum size for guided group; and three to five meetings per week of one to two hours duration have proven to be most productive. Each group within the Highfields concept proceeds through a series of stages in its development from an aggregate of approximately ten strangers to a closely knit primary group whose members are able to relate to one another in some significant way.

In the formative beginning of a group, there is little or no discernible group structure. The members engage in seeking information about one another, the group leader, and their environment; in testing the situation by engaging in hostile, defensive behavior, and by paying lip service to conventional standards.

The second stage is characterized by the development of an awareness of themselves and others, as well as the formation of cliques within the larger group. A clique is a subgroup of the total group. It is a defensive measure designed to protect the persons in the clique from the remainder of the group, including the group leader. Through mutually supportive interaction in the group sessions, the members of the clique can pretend to change their deviant behavior while actually avoiding such change. This is what is commonly known as "beating the program."

The cliques must be analyzed, discussed and broken by the total group before frank, honest and open discussion and resolution of all the problems of all the group members can occur. Deviant social roles and self-conceptions are revealed at this time, and a great deal of tension is generated around revealing one's feelings about other members.

The third stage is the critical period. The clique ties are broken and identification with the larger group is demanded. The sessions are characterized by an expression of intense hostility, particularly toward the group leader; defenses are breached and much frustration is experienced. The outcome of this struggle is a high degree of group solidarity and mutual identification. Also involved in this process is the idea of reforming one's self by attempting to reform others. The group member accepts the common purpose of the group, identifies himself closely with other persons engaged in reformation, and assigns status to others on the basis of conventional behavior.

The final stage is a relatively short period of intense, constructive activity. There is a direct assault on each member's problems, and an expression in action of confidence in the group's ability to resolve any difficulty. There is a minimal dependence on the group leader. The members review each other's roles, interpersonal relationships, and past and present behavior.

AN EVALUATION OF THE IMPACT OF GUIDED GROUP INTERACTION

An evaluative look at the impact of guided group interaction was obtained several years ago when I conducted a simple research study of 50 boys in the three New Jersey residential group centers who were narcotic users. Narcotic users, as opposed to addicts, generally use drugs primarily as a means of sharing a social activity with others. Users generally do not become physiologically dependent upon drugs nor find it necessary to increase the dosage because their usage is a social activity, the initial goal of which is socialization rather than getting high. Some of these 50 boys had been admitted for using narcotics while others were admitted for other offenses, but also had a history of drug use. Although none of the boys were "hard core" drug addicts, a number of them had regularly experimented with heroin. The primary hypothesis being tested was that if the genesis of narcotic use among juveniles is largely a socialization process, then the residential group center program utilizing guided group interaction should be successful in its treatment of the juvenile drug user, since the orientation of guided group interaction is resocialization.

The post-release adjustment reports of the narcotic users were analyzed in order to determine the boys' status and the quality of their adjustment in the community a minimum of six months after leaving the centers.

From the original sample of 50 boys, reports were available on 38 boys, 5 did not complete the program successfully, i.e., they were classified as unsuitable and either ran away or were returned to juvenile court. The remaining 7 had not been in the community for the minimum period of 6 months necessary to assess their adjustment. The findings are shown in Table 7–I.

The table shows that 76.5 percent of the users could be termed successes. Of these, 37 percent, or better than one in three, made good adjustments. Although 23.5 percent committed new offenses, only 13 percent were considered serious enough to warrant commitment to the reformatory. Thus, 87 percent, with varying degree of adjustment, were still in the free community.

PROBLEMS OF RUNAWAY YOUTH

TABLE 7-I
POST-RELEASE ADJUSTMENT OF NARCOTIC USERS

Adjustment	Number	Percent
Good	14	37
Average	15	39.5
Poor (New Offenses)	4	10.5
Very Poor (Committed to the reformatory)	5	13
Total	38	100

If the five boys classified as unsuitable for the Highfields program were included in the figures in Table 7–I, the results still indicated a favorable success rate by a comfortable margin. As shown in Table 7–II, 67.5 percent were successes, and 81.5 percent were in the community.

TABLE 7-II
POST-RELEASE ADJUSTMENT OF NARCOTIC USERS
INCLUDING UNSUITABLES

Adjustment	Number	Percent
Good	14	32.5
Average	15	35
Poor (New Offenses)	6	14
Very Poor (Committed to the reformatory)	8	18.5
Total	43	100

These figures reflect favorably upon the success of the residential group center program, and particularly guided group interaction, in its treatment of the juvenile narcotic user. Conceding the fact that the program was dealing with users rather than addicts, the results must still be impressive. Further, it is felt that these figures would be impressive when compared with those from any program dealing with narcotic users, juvenile or adult.

GROUP SIX—A CASE STUDY

In order to illustrate the foregoing overview, I wish to draw upon my own initial experience as assistant superintendent at New Jersey's Ocean Residential Group Center, for which Highfields was a prototype. One of my responsibilities was to conduct guided group interaction sessions. The description and assessment of the group which follows was my first experience with this technique.

Group Six came into existence as a group in July. The oldest member, in reference to length of stay, had arrived during the latter part of June. These and all other arrivals prior to the end of July were overlapping members in the previous group. In all, there were nine such overlapping members. Four boys arrived during the first week of August to give the group a total membership of thirteen. However, one boy ran away and was returned to juvenile court after one day in residence; and two other boys ran away after several weeks in residence, committed new offenses, and were subsequently sent to the reformatory. The fourth boy was returned to court as unsuitable, and he too was sent to the reformatory. Thus, the final size of Group Six was nine members.

Harry

The first boy in the group, HARRY, was seventeen years old. He was the oldest boy in reference to length of stay in the program. He had first been known to the juvenile court at the age of twelve when he was arrested for larceny and attempted breaking and entry. At this time, he was placed on probation for one year. He was dismissed from probation with improvement the following year.

At age fourteen he was again arrested on two counts of breaking and entry, and larceny, and multiple shoplifting. He was given a suspended sentence to the State Home for Boys and placed on probation for three years. Two years later he was again apprehended for shoplifting and his probation was continued. The following year he was discharged from probation with improvement.

At seventeen he was arrested and charged with three counts of breaking, entry, and larceny and breaking and entry. For these offenses he was given a suspended sentence to the Annandale Reformatory for Males and placed on probation for one year with the condition that he attend the Highfields program.

HARRY was Catholic, had three sisters, and his father was alcoholic. He had a poor school record and was a flagrant truant. His I.Q. tested at 97. He was characterized as being helpful at home, respectful of authority, but as having poor self-control.

Bill

The second oldest boy in the group, BILL was a somewhat weak and immature boy of eighteen. He had first appeared in court the previous year for possessing and drinking alcoholic beverages. In addition, he had committed numerous motor vehicle violations. BILL had been without a father for ten years and was not properly supervised by his mother who was employed on a full-time basis as the owner of a tavern. He had developed a serious drinking problem at a very young age.

BILL was ordered to the State Diagnostic Center at Menlo Park where his condition was diagnosed as "maladjustment reaction of adolescence with dissocial traits." The prognosis was good, but it was recommended that his needs for control, guidance and goals be met immediately. It was felt that he had to be shown "that he cannot get away with dictating his terms to the world around him, whether it be through ingratiation or through threats."

Eddie

EDDIE was a seventeen-year-old narcotics user from an upper middle class family consisting of his mother and step-father. He had previously been placed on unofficial supervision with improvement.

When last apprehended for larceny of doctors' bags, EDDIE admitted consuming such forms of barbiturates as Seconal, Miltown, Tuninal, and Nembutal over a period of two and a half years. For a period of six months, he also injected himself with Heroin, Morphine, Demerol, Morphine Acetate and Cocaine.

This boy possessed above average intelligence (I.Q. 121), and came from a good home. His probation officer characterized him in the following manner: "He lacks initiative, is irresponsible, and is content 'floating through life', being a crutch on his parents in particular, and society in general."

Art

The fourth oldest boy in the group, ART was seventeen. He lived with his mother and step-father who was an attorney. He had been apprehended on numerous occasions for motor vehicle larceny and driving without a license.

His commitment to the New Jersey State Diagnostic Center at Menlo Park resulted in the following report:

"Diagnosis: Personality Trait Disturbance, Emotional Immaturity.

Prognosis: In the present day setting he has missed too much school and possibly still has some reading disability to be able to pursue any career which would require some scholastic achievement. Pushing him in this direction will create further difficulties. Being volatile emotionally and immature he will be subjected to the influences of others and a similar act may be repeated. He, however, does not seem to be antisocial and aggressive.

Recommendation: . . . . The staff believes that at the present time probationary measures, referral to a Mental Hygiene Clinic and training in some trade such as auto mechanic while on probation is indicated. A provision to have him in a correctional institution should the offense be repeated is recommended as a deterrent."

Mike

MIKE, a sixteen-year-old boy, was admitted into the Highfields program for motor vehicle larceny and drunken disorderly conduct. He had first appeared in court the year before for possession of a stolen car, at which time he was adjudged delinquent and placed on probation.

MIKE later appeared in juvenile court for drunkenness and on charges of trespassing on property, continual annoyance of family, and breaking, entry and larceny. He had dropped out of school after having an extremely poor attendance record and being considered a behavior problem in school.

Much of MIKE's problem was considered to be his father's drinking and extremely neurotic behavior. Because of this and his mother's outside employment, family control was limited.

Most of his difficulties in the community occurred while he was involved in group activity. He was extremely desirous of peer group acceptance and would go to some lengths to attain it. He seemed to have little ability to be alone or direct himself.

Craig

CRAIG came from a family in which his siblings had a history of delinquency. The probation department felt that he was a follower who was easily misled into deviant behavior, and that he had little insight or control in regard to himself. Also, it was felt that his difficulties stemmed partly from a parental lack of concern and the fact that he was free to roam the streets and do as he pleased. CRAIG's previous history of delinquency indicated the offenses of breaking, entry, entry and larceny, disorderly, possession of alcohol, disorderly, consumption of alcoholic beverages, and escaping from the police headquarters.

CRAIG was a fairly quiet but tough "farm boy" type from a rural area. His delinquency was of a relatively unsophisticated but aggressive nature. The fact that he was relatively short, although muscular, and had previously lost one eye might indicate that his aggressiveness was partially compensatory.

Pete

PETE, age sixteen, first appeared in court on charges of larceny the previous year. He was later charged with sniffing glue, an offense which was committed numerous times. Members of his peer group were involved with him in these infractions. PETE's adjustment in school was very poor. His probation officer felt his offenses were the result "of a personal problem of the boy and his lack of understanding of himself." PETE appeared to resent his father and also had difficulty in adjusting to the type of community in which he was living.

George

GEORGE was involved in sniffing airplane glue on many occasions. He had also been apprehended for consumption of alcoholic beverages and was suspected in various automobile larcenies. He was seventeen years old at the time of his admission.

This boy had excessive group loyalties which were often detrimental to his own position and welfare, and he would not reveal any information to the police nor make any admissions. His parents had no understanding of his misbehavior and antisocial activities.

Lee

The youngest boy in the group was a husky, blond youth named LEE, who was nearly eighteen at the time of admission. His father was deceased and his mother was a medical secretary who was born in Germany.

For several years prior to his admission, LEE was involved in various breaking and entry charges and one runaway episode. His school work was barely passing and his most important interest was his fifteen year old girlfriend.

LEE was diagnosed as a constricted boy who felt little anxiety and bottled up his sense of inadequacy. He always managed to divorce himself from any real involvement with others. However, he was felt to be a boy capable of amiability, thoughtfulness, cooperativeness, and politeness, and his prognosis was generally favorable.

During the early stages, the group had no group structure. Instead, it was an aggregate of individuals basically divided into two factions. The four oldest boys, three of whom had arrived within a two-day period, constituted the first faction. The leader of this clique was a tough, aggresive, somewhat bullyish narcotic user named Rich, who for reasons to be described shortly was not considered a part of this group. His compatriots were HARRY, BILL and EDDIE.

The second faction was led by PETE. The other members of that clique were GEORGE and LEE. These three boys had been admitted together from the same county and thus knew each other prior to their arrival.

MIKE and CRAIG could be considered isolates in that they chose to remain aloof from all the other members of the group, whereas ART served as the scapegoat for the group, and was excluded from membership in both of the two factions.

The early sessions of Group Six consisted of hostile, defensive behavior, primarily on the part of Rich. Lip service to conventional standards came from HARRY and to some extent from EDDIE. The early sessions were primarily taken up by the telling of stories and the assignment of problems by the group. Telling stories means that each boy had to describe in detail to the group all the delinquent activities in which he had been involved, whether or not he had been caught for them. He also had to describe and discuss his relationships with his family, what he had done in school, etc.

Early in July, Rich and EDDIE brought narcotics into the facility, in the form of glue and barbiturates. Following a typical delinquent pattern, they refused to admit this either to the staff or to their group. Because of this they were returned to juvenile court. This was done to impress upon them the seriousness of their behavior and also to make an impact upon their group. They and their peers had to learn that in order for them to benefit from the program, it was absolutely necessary that they discuss their delinquency in the group sessions. This they could do and remain immune from punishment. This immunity must be maintained if the necessary trust relationship within the group is to be developed. The group must serve a rehabilitative and not a punitive purpose. After a period of time, Rich and EDDIE were returned to the program.

The group did not begin to develop a complete structure until the latter part of August when the oldest boys were already at the facility two months. It was also at this time that Rich was again returned to court as unsuitable for the program. This decision was made because Rich was obstructing the formation of a group structure and was interfering with the attempts of the other boys to help themselves and each other. He had not gained from his previous experience and had decided that he liked what he was and was not going to attempt to change. Occasionally a case arises in which a boy appears to be a suitable candidate for the program on the surface, but simply proves not to be amenable to this particular approach. In that case it is better to remove the individual than it is to allow him to destroy the necessary group culture.

As the group passed through the stage of revealing themselves and their feelings about each other, the members began to identify with their group and to recognize the fact that demands were being made upon them to help make group decisions. This was also the time during which the basic decision was made to change or not to change. ART was still divorced from the group, partly because of his low status and partly through his own choices.

As Group Six entered its third stage, Rich was gone. HARRY and BILL came more and more to assume the leadership of their group, partly because they were the two oldest boys. The lines were much less clearly drawn between the two cliques, and GEORGE was emerging as one of the most influential members of the group. The fundamental basis of influence in the meeting was changing from deviant to non-deviant, and BILL and GEORGE were making the greatest progress in that direction. MIKE and CRAIG became much more involved in their group.

Late in September, HARRY asked the group to discuss how he had solved his problems and his readiness to go home. HARRY believed that all his problems stemmed from his being easily "mislead," and because he had solved this he had solved his other problems as well. However, his reasons were weak and were not based, for the most part, upon what he had been doing at Ocean; therefore, they were rejected by the group. When the group did finally vote on HARRY's request, he received a "yes" vote from all but CRAIG who felt he didn't know enough about him. CRAIG's vote perhaps best told the story of HARRY and his progress toward solving his problems. HARRY never really did go beyond the plateau he had reached, but he was discharged in October. BILL was also discharged at the same time, but in his case a great deal of progress had occurred. An extract from his final monthly report indicates the following: "BILL had a good final month in residence at Ocean. His dependency and immaturity, very evident upon his arrival, all but disappeared during the latter part of his residence. He now seems very capable of dealing with all his problems and difficulties."

All the members of the group participated actively during this stage. They became genuine members of the group, and as this occurred, they were being alienated from previous delinquent group affiliations. ART was perhaps the only group member who didn't fall into this pattern. He was unpopular with and not accepted by his peers. He had no status and was consigned to remain a scapegoat. The group leader constantly had to interject himself in order to protect ART from being overwhelmed, and also to prevent the group from spending all its time discussing him and his problems.

An example of the group members' attempts to absolve themselves of previous delinquent associations was the case of MIKE. MIKE expressed the wish to have his buddies think he was the same old MIKE. He wanted to change and yet he wanted to remain the same. MIKE was being pressured by the group to make a choice between his old friends and new friends, i.e. between delinquency and nondelinquency.

In the final stage, Group Six directly attacked and resolved the problems of its members. ART was attacked for his lying, PETE on his use of narcotics, aggravation and "tough guy" problems, etc. During this period the leader performed only a minimal role, his major function being to sharpen the assault on the problems of group members and to emphasize the alternatives to delinquent behavior.

Role reversal was also evident during this last period, specifically between ART and CRAIG. These boys were unable to form a friendly relationship, but instead were constantly arguing, bickering, and becoming annoyed with each other. In order to alleviate this situation somewhat, the leader encouraged them to reverse roles, assume the identity of the other person, and attempt to see situations through the other person's eyes. This was accomplished with favorable results.

As the group accomplished its objectives, it began to send its members home. EDDIE and CRAIG left in November, and the remainder of the group in December. ART was the last to be discharged. Following are parts of the final reports on these boys. It should be noted that these reports are prepared for the boys and the group, and are presented orally to them. Certain points in the reports are included and phrased in a particular way for therapeutic impact.

Harry

"HARRY had an above average final month in residence at Ocean. . . HARRY's participation in the group sessions did not increase during his last month. He seemed to be content to mark time in order to find out what was going to happen to him. . . He became more involved with and more interested in helping his peers than at any other time during his stay."

Bill

"BILL had a good final month in residence at Ocean. His dependence and immaturity, very evident upon his arrival, all but disappeared during the later part of his residence. . . BILL is an active participant in the group sessions, and has played a big part in helping the other boys cope with their problems. He supports them when he feels they are right, but will attack them when he feels they are wrong. BILL's interest in doing this seems very sincere."

Eddie

"EDDIE's final month in residence was a vast improvement over his first three months. . . if he is sincere in his beliefs and attitudes, and his reasons are enough to keep him out of trouble on the outside, this is all that really matters. Only time will tell whether or not this is the case."

Mike

"MIKE had an above average fourth month in residence at Ocean. . . participation in the group sessions is erratic, which perhaps reflects his attitudes. His relationship with adults is good, and he is considered to be a good worker by his supervisors."

Craig

"Contrary to what he had shown previously, CRAIG indicated that he did know what was happening and that he had sound ideas and alternates for dealing with his problems and the problems of his peers. . . CRAIG became an active participant and even somewhat of a leader in the group sessions. His contributions were, for the most part, very worthwhile."

Art

"ART had an average final month in residence. In terms of what other boys were able to accomplish, ART's behavior and attitudes still left much to be desired. On the face of it, however, this boy appeared to progress as far as his capabilities would allow."

Pete

"PETE had an average final month in residence at Ocean. He doesn't seem to have made any great changes in his behavior and attitudes over his last reporting period. . . PETE participates actively in the group sessions and again is able to assume very well the role of a 'helped' boy. He becomes aggravated, vengeful, and then withdrawn when the group refuses to accept his ideas."

George

"GEORGE's active participation in the group sessions was directed sharply to the delinquent behavior and attitudes of the other boys. This was true to such an extent that GEORGE would become aggravated when his ideas and solutions were not readily accepted. It is in such situations that GEORGE's tendency to be a tough guy comes to the surface."

Lee

"LEE had a good final month in residence. His awareness of his own problems, and of the problems of other boys reached its highest point, and perhaps more important, his awareness of how to handle these problems became clearly evident. LEE was much involved with the other boys during his last month, and his change in attitude and behavior was clearly discernible."

ASSESSMENT OF GROUP SIX

In the brief, simplified look at the history of Group Six at Ocean, it is possible to see that the group did follow the different stages of development. Also, one can get an idea of how the group delineates, attacks, and finally solves the problems of its members.

During the group sessions, the leader attempts to support and assist the group in becoming aware of its problems, as well as to make interpretations of the interaction between members. Group members will openly and defiantly test the leaders' definition of the guided group interaction situation and his role in it. The hostile and aggressive reactions of the boys require a special type of leadership and ability. The leader usually handles aggressive reactions by turning them back to the group for their discussion. The leader's attitude must be one of acceptance, and he must not inflict punitive or counter-aggressive acts which would lead to condemnation of the boys themselves. He simply asks provocative questions, repeats ideas expressed in the group, and summarizes to bring out significant issues.

Turning to the role of the participants in guided group interaction, each person must, according to his ability, make some contribution to the maintenance of the group. They must be able to deal with each other, and work or exchange opinions with each other without hurting each other too much. This is very difficult to accomplish when the group has a scapegoat similar to ART who becomes a target.

Each person must evolve his own role in the group, understand his present role, and attempt to develop new roles. He must make the crucial choice that in order to survive in the community he must change his values, attitudes and behavior. Each member of the group learns that he helps himself by helping other group members.

Guided group interaction requires an easy, informal environment where members are democratic equals and where social controls evolve out of interaction and increased understandings. There are no formal rules or punishments imposed by the group leader, and the effort to establish such rules with accompanying punishments by the group itself should be discouraged. If allowed to develop, these can become the focus of the group's efforts rather than real behavior change. Rules and punishments can also become a method through which stronger group members subjugate weaker ones.

The sessions alone do not operate in a vacuum. There is a social world outside the meeting that is equally important in achieving the goals of the program. It is this outside social world that provides support for the meetings. The experiences provide the raw data for discussion of group and personal problems. Since the theoretical orientation of the program is focused on the "here and now" experiences of the boys and the people with whom they interact, every other kind of experience plays a part in the rehabilitation of the population. The informal norms and sanctions that govern social relationships should change with each group as it goes through the program.

As each boy leaves the residential group center, he is asked to record his impressions of his career, both in the community and in the program. Not all boys are able or willing to do so. However, most of the boys comply and prepare a statement of their impressions. The following stories were recorded by the boys in Group Six upon their release to the community. It is felt these will serve very effectively as a self-measure of the impact of the program upon the boys.

Harry

"My first impression of Ocean when I arrived was the same as everyone else's I presume. That is, being I had no thought of helping myself before I came here, I couldn't understand the boys that were here when I arrived. I couldn't see how they could look as if they were trying to help themselves when on the outside you never even dream of how seriously wrong you have been going about life. About what sorrows and regrets you are putting yourself through. But what's more is how the people you love and those who love and respect you are being affected by your wrong mistakes. And the people you do the wrong to are being very much affected by what you did to them. I am positive now though, that by being sent here is the best way of straightening out juveniles. Up here in Ocean you have the understanding and help of other boys and mainly the advantage of time to reason and think solely of the reasoning these other boys give you. I feel that on the outside there is no serious thinking and the time to really think because there is where all the temptations are and the way you are going about things will continue because of the temptations and unreasonable time. But as I have just said in a previous statement in this paragraph I am positive that here in Ocean is the best thing that can happen to a juvenile in the fact that here you have understanding help and reasonable time the reasons for leading a clean life."

Bill

"When I first came up to Ocean I looked around and knew this place wasn't for me. When I meet some of the kids I was almost sure that they were bullshiting. I didn't think that anybody could help themself. But I found out later that you could. So I tried to help myself and I did but I was sure went I first came up here that it couldn't be done. I am glad that I didn't go back to court. Now I think that this place is the best place for any boy that has gotten in trouble. When I leave this place I know that I will make good on the outside."

Eddie

"When I first came to Ocean I thought the place was big joke. I thought that all the guys were good-goodys and fags; and that they were all playing the role. I figures that this place couldn't help me or anybody else. The check system got me agrivated because I couldn't see any sense in it.

Now I feel that this place can help anyone who wants it to, it helped me. The check system, not only is good for making a person realize what he is doing but also for finding out what he is real like. The meetings are the main factor in helping people, because when a delinquent is told by another delinquent what he is doing wrong it means more than an adult. The one thing I disagree with is that this place is suppose to be run by the boys; but there is not one inclination of this. I think if the boys were given more of a chance to run the place, even in little ways, the boys might be able to be helped earlier. I feel that boys who come up here for drugs might be easily discouraged because the boys & the supervisors try to make them feel that drugs can not be helped. I feel that if the boys down here for drugs were given half a chance & not brainwashed into thinking they cannot be helped, more junkes could be helped. Another thing I disagree with is that Annandale is held over the boys head to much & this might force boys into playing the role. If other points were stressed more than Annandale less people would play the role which would lead into more people being helped. Something that gets me agrivated is the shit that a person in one meeting can't help a person in another meeting because he is said not to be interested in his own meetings. We are put up here to help us people, so why are we given hell for try to help each other? This deceiving us, & sometimes a person from a different meeting can be more of a help because of the simulating of their problems and background."

Mike

"When I first got here I thought the groups were a bunch of punks and good-goodies and this place wasnit the place for me but after a few days I found out different. I thought the check system was all fucked up. But after someone explained it I thought I would like to be helped so I went to work on it. Before I cam up I wanted to stay out of trouble but I went about it the wrong way on the outside. But being up here made me find out the right way to do this. I was told that the boys ran this place but later found out different. I thought that if you were voted out you would go home or on furlought but I guess not but that wasn't all that bad. I didn't mind the work at all because I liked most of it. I liked all the staff members except for Lead Ball. (A college student who spent the summer working as a seasonal assistant.) But that was my fault because I made a wise remark to him one day after that he disliked me. That taight me not to wise off. Also I disliked to do house cleaning. I also didn't think this place could help anybody that was what everybody said but I found out different.

I changed my ways of thinking altogether now. I think just about any body can be helped if they really want to help themselves. After being here a week or so I learned how to go about helping myself and how it changed me. I was talking to my probation officer and he noticed a change in me. I was only about 1 month old so that made me feel good. My parents saw a change also. I think this place is run about the best way it could be run and I don't think if a person can't be helped, there is no other place that can help him. I think Mr. Rose should be more strick on the boys because they are taking advantage of him to much. (Joy Rose was the Work Supervisor at the Ocean Residential Group Center.) By asking for cigarette breaks and so on. Otherwise I think everything is run alrite. I don't think it is his fault because he is trying to be a nice guy but instead he is getting fucked around. I think the whole programe set me up for my future because I have a lot more risonsibility now. In many way work, and being a good respictible person. I think I can do that now. So I think that this place is the only type of institution that is of any help to a delinquent and that places like Jamesburg and Annandale are no good to reform a person. I think they only make you worse than wat you were when you first got into trouble. I think that the meetings do the most for a boy because if you think something is minor like I did the meeting can change that because it did for me. I think the meeting can change almost anything that has to do with delinquency even late shit."

Craig

"The first Cuple Weeks Here.

"Well the day I arrived, I thought this place was a little cookie, I mean to me everybody was playing the roll. Everytime I did something rong someone was always checking me, at the time I didn't really know it was for my own good, I though they were trying to get me into trouble. When they would talk to me I would get wise, and try to start a fight with them. I though in my own mind people were trying to mess me up. The reason why I though this place was faged out when I came here is because the guys were checking me for everything I did rong. and because I couldn't clown around. I always used to clown and I wasn't used to stoping. Well I can't think of any more to say for the first cuple weeks.

The Rest of my time Here.

Well after I found out people were trying to help me. it made me think a lot about this place. I never paid attenchen in the meeting for a long I never said anything because I was afride I would get someone in trouble. But when I was a month an a half people were trying to help me. the talk problems with me. So I decided to try in help my self. I think matter in fack I got all my problems solved except for the following.

Clown. The reason why I didn't get my clown problem solved, is sertain times I feel I half to clown around with someone. to keep me out of bad moods and maybe get some one else out of bad moods.

Wise. Sure I get wise but when I get wise I think in my own mind it is helping me from getting aggervated at anyone. Other times I do it to clown. thata shy I know I didn't solve my wise guy problems, but as far as my other problems are concerned I did solve them. and I want to thank my meeting for helping me do it. and I am going to do my best to shown then I am helped. I want to thank mister Fincken- hawer and mister Reagon for everything they did for me. (Vincent J. Regan was the Superintendent of the Ocean Residential Group Center at this time.) they are the two nicest guy you ever want to meet. Well that all I half to say."

Art

"When I first came here I thought that this place was pretty nice because to me it was a hundred percent better than county jail. But after awhile I started hating the place because everybody found out what I really am and that meant that they knew I was a liar and they were getting on my back quite a lot about it and I was getting quite aggrivated because I didn't want to tell anybody I was lying because I was ashamed about it and I didn't want to confess about it because I thought everybody would look down on me. But the thing that really made me start liking the place is that I started realizing that everybody was really trying to help me and when they had proof I was lying they tried to help me instead of teasing the hell out of me. I feel that the system this place has is very good because the people here make me think a lot and go by my own decisions. I feel that if it wasn't for this place I wouldn't have had enough courage to make my own decisions because I would be scared to mess myself up, loke on a job. For a while I thought to myself that Mr. Regan was just playing a hard tough roll, but now I realize that if I couldn't have taken it from Mr. Regan I couldn't have taken it from a boss on a job. Actually though, even though I don't express myself to well, I'm very grateful to Mr. Regan for what he did to me because he taight me the true meaning of responsibility by giving me punishment when I couldn't except responsibility. He and all the other members of the staff taught me to think for myself and to think before I do something. I feel that my main reason of why I got into trouble is because I never thought about the consiquences and I never thought about other people because I just wanted to be a big shot and show off in front of everybody. However, I found out from this place that I can get along just as well with people just by being my normal self. I feel that in a way I owe my future to all the people here because thier the ones that really made me change my mind to change my ways and begin a new beginning. I only hope that a lot of other kids get the break I got."

Pete

"When I first arrived at Ocean I thought I knew pretty much about the place. I was wrong. My opinion about the older boys was that they were playing the role and I couldn't be changed.

My opinion of the place really changed when I was about two months old on my second furlough. I drank and after I drank I was mad at myself from then on my reasons had a lot more meaning. I did at times act good just for the sake of looking good, but, I'm leaving with greater confidence in myself with an honest pity on my friends and my brother who get in trouble. I used to think they were great but now I feel sorry for them."

George

"When I first came up here I wanted to be helped but the way they went about it didn't go over to well. With its check system and the work I never had a job on the outside cause I was to lazy to go out and work now I think I can do better on the outside cause of this experience.

When I first came here I didn't get along with everyone to well I had a big mouth I got agravated real easy and I didn't like people to say stuff like critizing me this was the hardest thing so solve I didnt solve it all the way but I realized what I was doing and I soped. Then some of the guy I didnt get along with I started getting along with better I think this is a pretty important thing in life, getting along with people.

This place started me doing something I never did be for giveng in and exepting critizism with out getting pissed off at people.

I didnt have a flunky problem but Mr. Regan pointed out something that stoped me from some future bust. he remarked on how I used to get mixed up in my friends quarrels.

Some thing else mr finkenhuaer said in arty about there are problemes are all naginfied in arty then I though about it and it made sence so I tried to change those things.

When I get on the outside Im going to hang around with my friend who dont get busted cause that way I can never get pushed or triped into any thing.

Another thining I could neve make the right dision so I was scard to make them now at least I try to think for my self.

I think my worst problems were my family and sniffing I going to get along better with my family now and I no Ill never sniff again I realize how stupid it was. my parent are alway worring about me no I going to worry about them."

Lee

"Most guys, when they first get here, think that they got a rotten deal by being sent here. I guess that's the way that I felt too but I realize now that these past four months have been the most important months of my life. I admit that Ive been slick, but I guess everyone has (and I'm not using that as an excuse thought I'm only saying what's on my mind). I've benefitted, and I think that most guys bene-fit from this program in one way or another. Unfortunately some guys benefit in the wrong way because some guys just don't want to go strat and nothing will ever change their minds. I think that if everyone was sent to this place there wouldn't be need for as many reforma-tories and jails as their are. I guess I don't have anything else to say, just that this place helped me and will always stay with me."

EPILOGUE OF GROUP SIX

Each boy released from the residential group centers is returned to probation status in the community, and a post release adjust-ment report is completed by his probation officer between six months and eighteen months following his release. Six months is considered to be the crucial time period for readjustment in the community.

The post release adjustment reports on the same boys in Group Six reflected the following:

Harry

HARRY did not appear in court for a new violation or offense fol-lowing his release, and was discharged from probation supervision with improvement. His overall adjustment was considered good and he was working full time. The probation officer felt that the experience of residence in the group center had been of definite value to HARRY.

Bill

BILL was discharged from probation without improvement, and his overall adjustment was considered to be poor although he had ap-parently committed no new violations or offenses. The probation officer felt that BILL's experience at the group center was of some value to him.

Eddie

EDDIE was committed to the New Jersey Reformatory for Males at Annandale about three months after discharge. He was charged with possession of narcotic paraphernalia and consorting with a narcotic user. Seven months later EDDIE was recalled from Annandale by the juvenile court judge and continued on probation. At that time he enrolled as a 12th grade student in the local high school.

Mike

MIKE was still under probation supervision at the time of the report. He had appeared in court again for drunkenness on six occasions, and was being treated at the New Jersey Neuro-Psychiatric Clinic. Despite these problems, his overall adjustment following release from the group center was considered good, and the probation officer felt that his experience had been of definite value to MIKE.

Craig

CRAIG was still under probation supervision at the time of the report. He had appeared in juvenile court again for possession of alcohol, and his probation was continued. His overall adjustment was considered good; he was working part time; and he was actively seeking additional employment. The probation officer felt that the experience of residence in the group center had been of definite value to CRAIG.

Art

ART was committed to the Annandale Reformatory for auto theft three weeks after his release from Ocean. He had returned to Ocean on a Sunday evening approximately two weeks after his discharge for a visit. At that time he was driving a second hand car which he indicated had been bought for him by his father. Although he emphasized how well he was doing, he seemed nervous and apprehensive, particularly when he voluntarily explained in detail about the car. It was discovered later that the car in fact had been stolen, and ART was committed for this theft on the following Friday. It seems, in retrospect, almost as if he were reaching out for help and wanted to be challenged and helped in his wrongdoing just as he had in the guided group sessions.

After serving a period of time at Annandale, ART, while on a preparole release status during his final month was assigned the task of painting the home of the assistant superintendent, along with several other boys. The other boys apparently talked ART into running away.

He was caught and subsequently committed to the Bordentown Reformatory for Males (an institution for older, more sophisticated offenders).

Representing one of the two most evident failures from this group, ART's inability to resist being misled and to adhere to socially acceptable behavior would point toward evidence of psychopathic tendencies. Because of this, the guided group sessions did not impact upon him except on a superficial level. He was able to verbalize the characteristics of a "helped" boy as evidenced by his self-description, but he was not able to behave accordingly. ART represents a good example of the need in the groups to get below this superficial level and to divert into another type of treatment effort those who cannot profit from guided group interaction.

Pete

PETE was still under probation supervision and had appeared in juvenile court again for possession of beer. His probation had been continued at that time. PETE's overall adjustment was considered to be good and he was attending school at the time of the report. The officer felt that PETE's experience had been of definite value to him.

George

George was under probation supervision at the time of the report. He had been charged with assault and was scheduled to appear in New York Criminal Court. Although he had reenrolled in school, he again dropped out and was currently working full time. The probation officer felt he had made an average overall adjustment, and that the group center had been of some value to GEORGE.

Lee

LEE had violated probation for an unstipulated offense and was continued on probation. His overall adjustment following release from the group center was considered very good. He was attending school and working part time. The probation officer felt that the experience of residence in the group center had been a definite value to LEE.

With the exception of the two obvious failures, EDDIE and ART, and despite some other more or less marginal adjustments, the consensus of opinions of the probation officers who supervised these boys before and after their group center experience was that it had been of value to them. This is a good example of the intangibles involved in changing human behavior. Significant changes in attitudes and outlook might occur even with occasional early relapses in behavior patterns. The post-release adjustment of the group is also a good example, and this is offered only partially as an excuse, of the results of inexperience and resort to trial and error learning on the part of the group leader.

The implications of the Highfields concept for the rehabilitation of young offenders cannot be over-emphasized. It may also be a progressive form of prevention for coping with predelinquents as well. New programs, utilizing guided group interaction, could be designed for this purpose and might open new avenues for the prevention and control of juvenile delinquency.

The operating model described has been successfully modified from time to time, so that each program develops features designed to meet its particular set of problems. However, the concept that the peer group can be used in effecting change in the attitudes and behavior patterns of adolescents must remain intact. Adolescents have the potential for change and for dealing with their own problems as well as the problems of others. The group approach using guided group interaction is one effective method for developing this potential.

REFERENCES

Elias, Albert: The Highfields program for juvenile delinquents. Unpublished report, March, 1961.

Elias, Albert: A reply to some unanswered questions about Highfields. *American Journal of Correction,* July –August, *21:* No. 4, 1959.

McCorkle, Lloyd W., Elias, Albert, and Bixby, F. Lovell: *The Highfields Story.* New York, Holt, 1958.

McCorkle, Lloyd W.: Group therapy in the treatment of offenders. *Federal Probation, 16:*22–27, 1952.

Sherwood, Clarence C., and Walker, William S.: Some unanswered questions about Highfields, University of Michigan Press, Ann Arbor, Michigan, 1959.

LANGUAGE OF THE DRUG ABUSER

Compiled by
JOHN G. CULL AND RICHARD E. HARDY

THIS SECTION OFFERS a glossary of the language of the drug user. The glossary is in no way complete, but every effort has been made to select those words and terms which may be used most frequently. The reader should remember that the use of these words varies dramatically among geographic regions. A word which is popular in one area may be used very seldom in another.

These words represent the word usage of many addicts throughout the country; however, it is doubtful that any one addict would be familiar with all the included terms.

The argot which addicts use gives a clear description of their way of life. From the terms the reader will be able to discern the compensatory use of drugs by the individual with an inadequate personality and the necessity for many users for escape from reality. Many of the words in the language of the addict are words or modifications used originally by opium smokers, and a number of these words are oriental in origin.

If professionals are to be of help to members of the drug culture, they not only must understand the language of the drug abuser but also must have a feeling for the differences in his perceptions of words and his use of language. Work done by the authors (Cull and Hardy, 1973a; Cull and Hardy, 1973b; and Hardy and Cull, 1973) indicate subcultural groups use language in decidedly different fashions. Racial differences and differences in physical capacities cause individuals to use and perceive everyday language in an altered fashion. Consequently, professionals who work with drug abusers must understand the jargon of this group. This glossary is only the first step in developing this understanding.

A

Abe—A Five-Dollar bill.
Acapulco Gold—A high quality of Marijuana.
Acid—LSD (Lysergic Acid Diethylamide). Hallucinogen.
Acid Dropper—One who uses LSD.
Acid Freak—A habitual user of LSD, Cube Head.
Acid Head—LSD user.
Action—The selling of narcotics. Anything pertaining to criminal activities.
Alcohol—Booze, Juice.
Amp.—A 1 cc Methedrine Ampule, legitimate.
Amphetamines—Stimulants which are generally Dexedrine, Benzedrine, Methedrine, or Biphetamine. Bambita, Bennies, Bottles, Browns, Cartwheels, Chicken Powder, Co-pilots, Dexies, Eye openers, Footballs, Greenies, Hearts, Jolly Beans, Jugs, LA Turnabouts, Lid Proppers, Orangies, Peaches, Pep Pills, Roses, Speed, Truck Drivers, Ups, Wake Ups, Whites.
Amys—Amyl Nitrate, Stimulant.
Angel Dust—PCP, an animal tranquilizer.
Artillery—Equipment for injecting drugs.
Away—In jail.
Axe—Musical Instrument.

B

Back up—A condition in which blood backs up into the syringe while injecting a drug into the vein.
Backtrack—To make sure a needle is in proper position when mainlining by withdrawing the plunger of the syringe before actually injecting the drugs.

Bad Trip—Bummer.

Bag—Situation; category.

Bag—An envelope of Heroin (see Nickel Bag and Dime Bag).

Bagman—An individual who sells drugs.

Bambita—Desoxyn or Amphetamine Derivative.

Bambs—Barbiturates.

Band House—Jail.

Bang—Fix, shot; injection of narcotics.

Barbiturates—Sedatives, usually Seconal, Nembutal, Amutal, Luminal, Tuinal. Barbs, Blue Heavens, Double Trouble, Nimbie, Peanuts, Purple Hearts, Rainbows, Red Devils, Sleeping Pills, Yellow Jackets.

Barbs—Barbiturates.

Bay State—A standard medical hypodermic syringe, usually made of glass with metal reinforcement, using a plunger and screw-type needle.

Bean Trip—Intoxication from ingesting Benzedrine; a Benny Jag.

Beat—To cheat or out bargain.

Bee that stings—A drug habit, especially one coming on; "a monkey on my back."

Belt—The euphoria following an injection of narcotics. A shot, or a quantity of drugs to be injected.

Bennies—Benzedrine.

Benny Jag—Intoxication from ingesting Benzedrine.

Bernice—Cocaine.

Bhang—Marijuana. See Cannabis.

Big C—Cocaine.

Big D—LSD.

Big John—The police or any law enforcement officer.

Bindle—A small package of narcotics.

Bit—A prison sentence.

Black and White—A policeman.

Black Beauty—Speed in a black capsule.

Blackjack—Paregoric which has been cooked down to be injected in a concentrated form.

Blank—Bag of nonnarcotic powder sold as a regular bag (also Dummy, Turkey).

Blanks—Gelatin capsules supposedly filled with a drug which are actually filled only with milk powder or sugar powder or sugar cubes supposedly saturated with LSD which have only food color.

Blasted—Under the influence of drugs.

Blast Party—Group gathered to smoke Marijuana.

Blotter—A piece of absorbent paper on which LSD has been absorbed.

Blow—To lose something; to smoke Marijuana.

Blow a Pill—To smoke Opium.

Blow a Stick—To smoke a Marijuana cigarette.

Blow Snow—To sniff Cocaine.

Blow Weed—To smoke Marijuana.

Blue Birds—Blues, Barbiturates.

Blue Devil—Amobarbital sodium in solid blue form.

Blue Heavens—Barbiturates.

Blue Mist—A sugar cube colored blue by an LSD preparation.

Blues—Barbiturate.

Blue Velvet—Sodium Amytal, Pyribenzamine.

Bombido—Injectible Amphetamine (Also Jugs, Bottles).

Boost—Steal.

Booster—A professional shoplifter, male or female.

Boot—Pushing and pulling the plunger of a syringe to cause a "rush."

Booze—Alcohol.

Bottles—Injectible Amphetamines.

Boy—Heroin.

Bread—Honey.

Brick—A kilogram of Marijuana compressed under pressure to retain the shape of a brick.

Browns—Long acting Amphetamine Sulfate (capsules, many colors mainly brown).

Buffotenine—A drug chemically related to DMT derived from dried glandular secretions of certain toads as well as from the *amanita* fungus.

Bug—To annoy.

Bum Beef—False complaint or information which usually is given deliberately to the police.

Bum Kick—Boring, unpleasant.

Bum Rap—An arrest or conviction for a crime the man actually did not commit, as distinguished from denying it.

Bum Steer—See Bum Beef.

Bum Trip or Bummer—A bad trip on LSD.

Bundle—Twenty-five $5 bags of Heroin.

Burned—Rendered useless or vulnerable by recognition; e.g. "A narcotic agent was *burned* and unable to continue surveillance." Also, to receive nonnarcotic or highly diluted drugs.

Bust or Busted—Arrested; broke.

Buttons—See Mescaline.

Buy—A narcotic peddler; a purchase of narcotics.

C

Caballo—Heroin.

Cactus—See Peyote.

Cactus Buttons—See Mescaline.

Can—A car; A city Jail.

Candy—Barbiturates.

Cannabis—Known variously as Bhang, Charas, Dagga, Ganja, Kif, Macoha, and Marijuana.

Cap—A person, especially a young Black, who has to hustle to support his habit. Also, a gelatine capsule or a capsule of drugs.

Cartwheels—Amphetamine Sulphate in round, white, double-scored tablets.

Cat Nap—To get small (and very welcome) snatches of sleep during the withdrawal period.

Chalk—Methedrine.

Charas—Marijuana. See Cannabis.

Charged Up—Under the influence of drugs.

Charley—Cocaine.

Charley Coke—A Cocaine addict (restricted to New York and New England).

Chicago Leprosy—Multiple abscesses.

Chicken Out—Cop out.

Chicken Powder—Amphetamine powder.

Chip—Heroin.

Chipping—Taking narcotics occasionally.

Chippy—Nice-looking girl.

Chloral Hydrate—Joy juice.

Clear up—To withdraw from drugs.

Clout—To steal, especially as a shoplifter.

Coasting—The sensation of euphoria following the use of a drug. Used of all drugs except Cocaine. Serving an easy prison sentence.

Coast-to-Coast—Long-acting Amphetamine Sulphate in round forms found in many colors. Also LA turnabouts, Co-pilots, Browns.

Cocaine—Bernice, Big C, Charley, Coke, Corine, Dust, Flake, Girl, Gold Dust, Happy Dust, Heaven Dust, Her, Ice, Snow, Star Dust, White Nurse.

Codeine—School Boy.

Cohoba—Powdered seeds used as snuff.

Coke—Cocaine.

Coked Up—Under the influence of Cocaine.

Cold Turkey—Sudden withdrawal without any alleviating drugs.

Come Down—The end of a trip; the depressed feeling when the drug effects are fading.

Connection—A drug supplier.

Contact—A person who has a connection or who knows a supplier of drugs.

Cooker—Bottle top or spoon used for dissolving Heroin in water over flame.

Cook-It-Up—To prepare Heroin (or other Opiates) for injection by heating it in a cooking spoon.

Cool—(adj.) In complete control.

Cool—(v) To wait.

Cop a Fix—To obtain a ration of Narcotics.

Co-pilots—Amphetamines. Also Truck Drivers, Bennies.

Cop or connect—To buy or get; to purchase drugs.

Cop-out—To inform; to pull out or chicken out; to confess; to alibi.

Cop to—Admit to stealing.

Corine—Cocaine.

Cotton—The small wisp of cotton placed in the cooking spoon and used as a filter when the solution is drawn up into the needle.

Cotton Head—A narcotics abuser who depletes his supply of Narcotics and attempts to secure one more injection by re-cooking the cotton used from previous fixes.

Crackling Shorts—Breaking into cars.

Crank—Methedrine; stimulant.

Crash—An unpleasant ending of a trip.

Crash Pad—Apartment set up specifically for people to sleep in.

Crib—One's home or apartment. A house of prostitution. A hypochondriac with many persistent symptoms.

Croaker—Unscrupulous doctor who sells drugs or prescriptions to illicit drug users.

Crutch—Device used for holding shortened butt of Marijuana cigarette. See Roach Clip.

Crystal—Methedrine. See Speed.

Cube—LSD on sugar cubes.

Cubehead—See Acid Freak.

Cut—The dilution of a narcotic with substances like lactose (milk sugar) or quinine, strychnine, etc., in order to increase the profit of the drug trafficker.

Cut Out—To leave a certain place.

D

"D"—LSD.

Dagga—See Cannabis.

Daisy—A male homosexual. Also Sissy, Queen, Sex Punk.

Dead—No action.

Deal—Sell narcotics to addicts.

Dealer—Anyone who buys or sells stolen goods. A peddler.

Dealing—Keeping on with whatever one is doing; selling dope.
Deck—Several bags of drugs.
Desoxyn—Amphetamine derivative.
DET—A chemically developed hallucinogenic drug; it has not been found occurring in nature.
Deuce—Two-dollar package of Heroin.
Dexies—Dexedrine, stimulant.
Dig—To understand; to follow.
Dime Bag—A $10 purchase of Narcotics.
Dirty—Possessing drugs, liable to arrest.
DMT—A hallucinogen found in the seeds of certain plants native to parts of South America and the West Indies. The powdered seeds have been used for centuries as a snuff "Cohoba."
Dollies—Dolophine; synthetic Heroin.
Dolly—Methadone.
Dolophine—Dollies, synthetic Heroin.
DOM or STP—(4-Methyl-2, 5-Dimethoxyamphetamine) A hallucinogenic drug produced in the laboratory which induces euphoria and other hallucinogenic effects.
Doo Jee—Heroin.
Dope—Narcotics. Information. To drug. This term, like dope fiend, tends to be taboo among addicts, though they use both perjuratively.
Dope Hop—A prison term for drug addicts, mostly used by guards, turn-keys, and police.
Double Trouble—Amobarbital Sodium combined with Seconbarbital Sodium in red and blue capsules.
Down—Basic; depressed.
Downer Freak—A habitual user of "Downers."
Downers—Sedatives, Alcohol, Tranquilizers and Narcotics.
Dragged—A post Marijuana state of anxiety.
Drop—Swallow a drug.
Dropped—Taken orally.
Dry—Without drugs.
Dummy—A bag of nonnarcotic powder sold as a regular bag. Also Blank, Turkey.

Dust—Cocaine.
Dynamite—Something extra special or good.

E

Echos—See Flashback.
Eighth—Eighth of an ounce of Heroin.
Electric—Overpowering, this is a positive statement.
Eye Dropper—Medicine dropper used with hypodermic needle as makeshift syringe. Most addicts actually prefer it to a syringe.
Eye Opener—Amphetamines.

F

Fag—A pimp. Not to be confused with the general slang fag (a homosexual) clipped from faggot.
Fall—To be arrested. To receive a prison sentence. See Bust.
Fat Jay—A Marijuana cigarette approaching the size of a commercial cigarette or larger. They are made large to compensate for weaker types of Marijuana.
Fed—A federal agent, usually a narcotic agent. Also, The Man, Narco.
Finger—Stool pigeon.
Finger Gee—Stool pigeon.
Finger Wave—A rectal examination for contraband narcotics.
Finif or Finski—A $5 bill.
Fink—A stool pigeon; an untrustworthy person. Also wrong, no good, rat.
Five-cent Bag—A $5 Heroin Fix.
Fix—Injection of Narcotics.
Flake—Cocaine.
Flash—A quick jolt of high in abdomen or across chest from Heroin shot.
Flashback—Partial reoccurrence of an LSD trip.
Flea Powder—Grossly inferior Heroin.

Flipped—Becoming psychotic after an overdose of drugs.

Floating—To be high on drugs.

Fly—Sophisticated yet carefree; wise in the ways of the underworld.

Flying—See Floating.

Footballs—Amphetamine sulphate in oval-shaped tablets of various colors. Also Greenies.

Fox—Good-looking girl.

Freak—An individual who is excessive in some area; for example, "Acid Freak" or "Speed Freak."

Freak-out—Bad experience with hallucinogenic drugs.

Fuzz—Policeman or Detective.

G

Gal Head—Narcotics addict.

Ganja—Marijuana. See Cannabis.

Garbage—See Flea Powder.

Gee Stick—An Opium Pipe. Obsolescent.

George—Very good.

Get a finger wave—The process of having the rectum searched for drugs.

Gig—Job.

Girl—Cocaine.

Give Wings—To start someone else on Narcotics.

Going Up—Taking drugs, particularly "Uppers."

Gold Dust—Cocaine.

Gold Leaf Special—A Marijuana cigarette which is thought to be very potent.

Goods—Narcotics, especially as they are bought and sold. Used by addicts or dealers in letters, phone calls, or telegrams.

Goof Balls—Barbiturates.

Goofers—See Goof Balls.

Gow—Narcotics in general, especially those used hypodermically.

Grapes—Wine.

Grass—Marijuana.

Greenies—Amphetamine Sulphate (oval shaped tablets).

Green Score—Profit made by passing counterfeit money.

Gun—Hypodermic needle for injecting Heroin.

H

"H"—Heroin.

Hack—A physician.

Hairy—Heroin.

Hang Tough—Take it easy, quiet down, stop.

Hang Up—A problem, generally a personal problem or a psychological problem.

Happy Dust—Cocaine.

Hard Stuff—Narcotics.

Harpoon—The hollow needle used with a joint. Also Spike, Silver Serpent, Pin, Machine, Tom Cat.

Harry—Heroin.

Hashish or Hash—Marijuana.

Hawk—LSD.

Hay—Marijuana.

Head—A user of drugs. Usually a user of LSD.

Hearts—Dexteamphetamine Sulphate in orange-colored heart-shaped tablets. Also Orangies, Dexies, Peaches, Bennies, Roses.

Heat—Police or Detective.

Heaven Dust—Cocaine.

Heavy—Deep or profound.

Heeled—See Dirty.

Hemp—Marijuana.

Henry—Heroin.

Her—Cocaine.

Heroin—Boy, Caballo, Doo Jee, "H," Hairy, Harry, Henry, Horse, Joy Powder, Junk, Scag, Scat, Skit, Smack, Stuff, Tecata, White Lady, White Nurse.

High—Under the influence of drugs.

Hip—Aware.

Hit—To shoot a narcotic.

Hit On—To ask for.

Hog—PCP.

Holding—See Dirty.

Holding—Having drugs in one's possession.

Hooked—Addicted.

Hooker—Hustler, a Prostitute.

Hop—Opium for smoking. Narcotics for injection or inhalation.

Hophead—Hype; a drug addict.

Hopped Up—Under the influence of Narcotics.

Horse—Heroin.

Hot Shot—Cyanide or other poison concealed in Narcotics to kill a troublesome addict.

Hump—To work.

Hustling—Activities involved in obtaining money to buy drugs.

Hype—Drug addict; Hophead.

I

Ibogaine—Derived from the roots, bark, stem, and leaves of an African shrub.

Ice—Cocaine.

Ice Cream Habit—See "Chipping."

Idiot Juice—Nutmeg and water mixed for intoxication, largely used in prisons.

Indian Hay—Marijuana.

Informer—Stool; an addict assisting police in arresting peddlers.

Iron Horse—A city jail. Most other underworld terms (Can, Joint, Band House, etc.) are also used by addicts.

J

"J"—A joint of Marijuana.

Jag—Under the influence of Amphetamines.

Jailhouse High—A high obtained from eating nutmeg.

Jeff—To be obsequious, especially Negroes in relation to Whites.

Jive— (adj.) —Worthless.

Jive— (n) Marijuana.

Joint—A Marijuana cigarette. The prison.
Jolly Beans—Amphetamines.
Joy Juice—Chloral Hydrate.
Joy Pop—Pse of Heroin in small amounts occasionally.
Joy Powder—Heroin.
Jugs—Injectible Amphetamines.
Juice—Alcohol.
Juice Head—An Alcoholic.
Junk—Narcotics, usually Heroin.
Junker—A Narcotic Addict.
Junkie—Narcotic Addict.

K

Key—One kilo of Marijuana.
Kick—Stop using Narcotics through complete withdrawal.
Kick Back—The addicts almost inevitable return to Narcotics after having kicked the habit.
Kick Cold—Treatment in which the addict is taken off drugs suddenly.
Kif—See *Cannabis.*
Kilo—A large amount of Narcotics from a pusher's point of view; technically 2.2 pounds. See Key.
Knockers—The testicles. A woman's breasts.
Knock Out Drops—Chloral Hydrate.

L

LA Turnabouts—See Coast-to-Coast.
Lamb—The passive receptor in a homosexual relationship.
Lame—Square.
Laughing Grass—Marijuana.
Lay Dead—To do nothing.
Lemonade—See Flea Powder.
Lettuce—Money.
Lid—A small quantity of Marijuana, usually about one ounce.

Lid Proppers—Amphetamines.
Lipton Tea—See Mickey Finn.
Lit—Under the influence of drugs.
Lit up—Under the influence of drugs.
Load—See "Deck."
Loco Weed—Marijuana.
Long-tailed Rat—Stool Pigeon.
Louse—A Stool Pigeon. (Also Finger, Finger Gee, Longtailed Rat. Mouse, Rat).
LSD—Acid, sugar cubes, trips. Lysergic Acid Diethylamide. Big "D." Hawk.
Luminal—A Barbiturate.

M

"M"—Morphine.
Machine—See Harpoon.
Macoha—See Cannabis.
MDA—Synthetic stimulant and hallucinogen.
Made—Recognized for what you are.
Main Line—(n) The vein, usually in the crook of the elbow, into which the needle addict injects Narcotics.
Main Line—(v) To inject Narcotics directly into a vein.
Maintain—Keeping your head during a difficult situation.
Maintaining—Injecting a Narcotic directly into a vein.
Mandrix—See Methaqualone.
Manicure—Marijuana with everything removed except the leaves.
Marijane—Marijuana.
Marijuana—Bhang, Cannabis, Charas, Ganja, Grass, Hash, Hashish, Hay, Hemp, Indian Hay, Jive, Laughing Grass, Loco Weed, Marijane, Pot, Railroad Weed, Reefer, Rope, Tea, Texas Tea, Weed.
McCoy—Medicinal drugs in contrast to bootleg drugs.
Medical Hype—A person who has become accidentally addicted during medical treatment for illness or disease; one who obtains bonafide drugs through doctors or hospitals.

Mellowing—The period of a crash when a person is on Speed.

Melsedin (In England)—see Methaqualone.

MESC—Mescaline; hallucinogenic drug derived from the bottoms of the Peyote cactus plant native to Central America and Southwestern United States. (Also Peyote).

Meth—Methedrine, or Methadone.

Methadone—Dolly, Dolophine Amidone.

Methaqualone—An addictive, sedative, hypnotic drug. See Mandrix, Melsedin (In England), Optimil, Parest, Quaalude, "Soapers", Sopor, Strasenburgh's Tuazole (In England).

Mickey—Chloral Hydrate.

Mickey Finn or Mickey—Chloral Hydrate in a drink to knock out a victim. Also euphemistically, Lipton Tea. A powerful physic such as croton oil, slipped into a whiskey to make the victim sick or to drive him away from a hangout.

Mike—A microgram.

Miss Emma—Morphine.

Mojo—Narcotics of any kind in a contraband trade; but usually Morphine, Heroin or Cocaine.

Monkey—A drug habit involving physical dependence.

Monkey on my back—Early abstinence symptoms. A drug habit.

Morphine—Hard Stuff, "M," Miss Emma, Morpho, White Nurse, White Stuff, Unkie.

Morpho—Morphine.

Mother—An individual's drug peddler.

Mouse—A Stool Pigeon.

Mr. Twenty-Six—A needle (refers to the gauge of the needle).

N

Nailed—To be arrested.

Narc or Narcos—The law; narcotic agent.

Nedle Fiend—An addict who gets pleasure from playing with the needle by inserting an empty needle for the psychological effect.

Needle Freak—One who enjoys using the needle. See Needle Fiend.

Needle Habit—A habit which is satisfied by hypodermic injections.

Needle Park—To New York addicts, upper Broadway and Sherman Square.

Needle Yen—A desire for Narcotics taken hypodermically. A masochistic desire to mainline.

Nembies—Nembutal.

Nemmies—Nembutal.

Nickel—A $5 bag of Narcotics or Marijuana; also a five-year sentence.

Nickel Deck—Five-dollar package of Heroin.

Nimbie—Nembutal.

Nimbies—Nembutal (Pentobarbital).

Nimby—Nembutal (Pentobarbital).

Nod—To be sleepy from a dose of drugs.

Nut City—A mythical place in which anyone feigning insanity is said to live.

O

O. D.—An overdose of Narcotics.

Off—Off of drugs, not to be taking drugs at the present time.

Off Someone—To kill someone or to beat someone up.

On Ice—In Jail. To lie low or go out of sight temporarily. Wanted by the law.

On the Nod—Sleep from Narcotics.

OP—Opium.

Opiates—Narcotics. Generally either Opium, Morphine or Heroin.

Opium—OP.

Optimil—see Methaqualone.

Orange Owsley—See "Owsley Acid."

Orangies—Dexedrine (Dextroamphetamine, orange colored, heart-shaped tablets).

Out-of-it—Confused, disoriented, unknowing; also, an outside person who is not part of the drug culture.

Out There—Confused.

Overjolt—Overdose of Heroin.

Owsley's Acid—LSD (West Coast slang after the illegal manufacturer, Augustus Owsley Stanley, III).

Owsley's Blue Dot—See "Owsley's Acid."

O.Z.—One ounce of Marijuana.

P

Pack Heat—To carry a gun.

Pad—User's home; place where he shoots up.

Paid off in gold—Arrested by a Federal officer who flashes his gold badge.

Panic—Shortage of Narcotics on the market.

Paper—A legal prescription for drugs.

Parest—See Methaqualone.

PCP—Angel dust. Peace Pill. Hog.

Peace Pill—PCP.

Peaches—Amphetamine Sulphate in rose-colored, heart-shaped tablets. (Also Roses, Hearts, Bennies, Orangies).

Peanuts—Barbiturates.

Peddler—A seller of Narcotics.

Pep Pills—Amphetamines. Also, Wake-ups, Eye Openers.

Pet—The police.

Peter—Chloral Hydrate.

Petes—Chloral Hydrate.

Peyote—Mescaline.

P.G.—Paregoric.

Phat—Well put together.

Piece—One ounce of Heroin; a gun.

Pill Head—Addict on pills.

Pin—See Harpoon.

Pink Owsleys—See "Owsley's Acid."

Pinks—Seconal (Secobarbital Sodium).

Pipe—An Opium smoker.

Plant—Stash-cache of Narcotics.

Pluck—Wine.

P.O.—A parole or probation officer.

P.O.—Paregoric.

Pot—Marijuana.

Pratt or Prat—A hip pocket.

Psilocybin or Psilocyn—Hallucinogenic drugs derived from certain mushrooms generally grown in Mexico.

Purple Hearts—A Barbiturate.

Purple Owsley—See "Owsley's Acid."

Pusher—Seller or dealer of drugs.

Put On—To deceive by design; to make fun of or to mislead someone.

Put the croaker on the send—A "fit" or spasm staged by an addict to elicit sympathy.

Q

Quaalude—See Methaqualone.

Queen—Male homosexual.

Quill—Matchbook cover used to inhale Narcotics. Powdered drug is placed in fold.

R

Rags—Clothes.

Railroad Weed—Marijuana of poor quality.

Rainbow Roll—An assortment of vari-colored barbiturates, popular among addicts on the West Coast.

Rainbows—Amobarbital Sodium combined with Secobarbital Sodium in red and blue capsules. Also, Red and Blues and Double Trouble.

Rap—Talk.

Rat—Stool Pigeon.

R.D.—A Red Devil.

Red and Blues—See Rainbows.

Red Devils—See Reds.

Reds—Seconal. Secobarbital Sodium.

Reefer—Marijuana cigarette.

Riff—Train of thought.

Right On—Affirmation of a truth; encouragement or support.

Rip Off—Steal or purchase of false Narcotics.

Roach—Butt of a Marijuana cigarette.

Roach Clip—A device used to hold the butt of a Marijuana cigarette.

Rope—Marijuana. So called because when smoked it smells of burning hemp.

Roses—Benzedrine (Amphetamine Sulphate), rose-colored, heart-shaped tablets.

Rosy—Wine.

Run—Period of addiction.

Rush—The intense orgasm-like euphoria experienced immediately after injecting a drug. Also, Flash.

S

Sam—Federal Narcotic Agents.

Satch—A method of concealing or smuggling drugs into jails.

Satchel—A girl.

Scag—Heroin.

Scat—Heroin.

Scene—Where something is happening.

Schmeck—Heroin.

School Boy—Codeine.

Scortch—To abuse someone verbally and very severely.

Score—To find a source of drugs.

Script—A prescription written by a physician to obtain drugs.

Script Writer—A sympathetic physician; someone who forges prescriptions.

Seccy—Seconal (Secobarbital Sodium).

Seconal—Sleeping pill; depressant, Pinks.

Send it home—To inject Narcotics intravenously.

Serpent—See Harpoon.

Sewer—The vein into which drugs are injected.

Sex Punk—A male homosexual.

Shakedown—To be arrested or held without charges in order to persuade the addict to supply information to police.

Shank—Knife.

Shit—Heroin.

Shoot—See Maintaining.

Shooting Gallery—Place where several addicts gather to shoot dope.

Shoot Up—See Mainlining.

Short—Car.

Short Go—A small or weak shot.

Shrink—A psychiatrist or psychologist.

Shucking—Wasting time.

Shy—To prepare a pill of Opium for smoking.

Silver—See Harpoon.

Silver Serpent—See Harpoon.

Sissy—A male homosexual.

Sitter—An individual who is sophisticated in the use of drugs, who will oversee others who are on LSD to make sure they don't harm themselves.

Sixteenth Spoon—Sixteenth of an ounce of Heroin.

Skin—Cigarette paper used for a Marijuana cigarette.

Skin Popping—Injecting drugs under the skin.

Sleeping Pills—Barbiturates.

Smack—Heroin.

Smashed—High on drugs.

Sneaky Pete—Wine.

Sniff—To sniff Narcotics (usually Heroin, Cocaine, or Glue).

Snort—To sniff powdered Narcotics.

Snow—Cocaine.

Snowbird—A cocaine user.

Soapers—See Methaqualone.

Sopor—See Methaqualone.

Sound someone—To feel someone out.

Speed—Methamphetamine; any stimulant, especially Amphetamines.

Speedball—A cocaine-heroin combination.

Speeder—A user of Methamphetamine.

Speed Freak—An excessive user of Methamphetamine.

Speeding—Using Methamphetamine.

Spike—See Harpoon.

Splash—Methamphetamine.

Split—To leave a place, sometimes in haste.

Spot Habit—See "Ice Cream Habit."

Square—Lame.

Stable—The community of girls who prostitute for one pimp.

Star Dust—Cocaine.

Stash—A place to hide drugs or money; generally a place well hidden but readily available.

Steam Boat—A tube such as an empty toilet tissue roll which is used to increase the amount of smoke from a Marijuana cigarette going into the lungs in order to increase the effectiveness of the cigarette.

Steam Roller—See Steam Boat.

Stick—A Marijuana cigarette.

Stir—Prison.

Stoned—High on drugs.

STP—Hallucinogen; lasts for 72 hours.

Straight—An addict's feeling of well-being after taking drugs.

Strasenburgh's Tuazole (In England) —See Methaqualone.

Strawberries—An LSD preparation.

Strung-out—Confused.

Stuff—Heroin.

Sugar—Narcotics, generally Heroin.

Sugar Cube—This is quite often a vehicle for LSD, a drop of LSD is absorbed by the sugar cube before being taken.

Sunshine—An orange or yellow tablet of LSD reputedly to be of a very potent strength.

Swingman—A drug peddler.

T

T or T Man—A big man. A Federal agent, especially a "narco."

Take a Trip—Using LSD.

Take Off—To smoke. To rob a place, especially of Narcotics.

Taste—Small quantity of Narcotics usually given as a reward or favor.

Tea—Marijuana.

Tea Man—A marijuana user.

Tecata—Heroin.

Ten-cent Pistol—Bag containing poison.

Texas Tea—Marijuana.

THC—Synthetic hallucinogen; produces same effect as Marijuana. Tetra Hydro Cannabinol. The active ingredients in Marijuana.

The Man—Policeman or Detective.

Ticket—A dose of LSD.

Tie Off—Stopping circulation in order for veins to rise.

Tight—Close.

Tinge—See Flash.

Tired—Old or worn out.

Tom Cat—See Harpoon.

Tooies—Tuinal capsules. See Double Trouble.

Tracks—Scars along the veins after many injections.

Trap—Prison.

Travel Agent—A person who sells LSD.

Trey—Three-dollar bag of Narcotics; generally Heroin.

Tripping—Taking a hallucinating drug.

Tripping Out—Same as Tripping.

Truck Drivers—Amphetamines.

Tuanol—Sleeping pill; depressant.

Tuinal—A barbiturate. Also called Rainbows or Double Trouble.

Turkey—Clod or square. A bag of nonnarcotic powder sold as a regular bag.

Turn On—To be excited by; to get high on drugs.

TV Action—Euphoria from drugs.

U

Unkie—Morphine.
Uppers—Stimulants; Cocaine, Speed and Psychedelics.

V

Vegetable—A person who has lost all contact with reality due to drugs.
Very Outside—Extremely far out or weird.
Vet—A prison or jail physician.
Vines—Clothes.
Vipe—To smoke Marijuana.
Viper—A Marijuana smoker.

W

Wake Up—Morning shot.
Wake-ups—Amphetamines.
Wasted—Stoned or drunk.
Way Out—Incomprehensible. The best.
Weed—Marijuana.
Wheels—Car.
White Cross—A white tablet of Speed which is sectioned with a cross.
White Lady—Heroin.
White Nurse—A term used to cover Cocaine, Morphine or Heroin; but more often Morphine.
White Owsley's—See Owsley's Acid.
Whites—Amphetamine Sulphate in round, white double-scored tablets.
White Stuff—"M," Hard Stuff, Morphine.
Wig—Head, hair.
Wig Out—To become psychotic as a result of Narcotics.
Wine—Grapes, Pluck, Rosy, Sneaky Pete.
Wired—Addicted to a Narcotic drug.
Works—Equipment for injection of drugs.

Y

Z

Yellow Jackets—Nembutal, Barb, depressant. Phenobarbital Sodium in yellow capsule form.
Yellows—Nembutal.
Zonked—Under the influence of Narcotics.

REFERENCES

Cull, J. G., and Hardy, R. E.: A study of language meaning (gender shaping) among deaf and hearing subjects. *J Percep Mot Skills, 36:*98, 1973a.

Cull, J. G., and Hardy, R. E.: Language meaning (gender shaping among blind and sighted students.) *J Psychol, 83:*333–334, 1973b.

Hardy, R. E., and Cull, J. G.: Verbal dissimilarity among black and white subjects: a prime concern in counseling and communication. *The Journal of Negro Education, XLII:*1, 67–70, 1973.

GUIDELINES FOR ESTABLISHMENT OF A HOTLINE SERVICE

GERALD R. BISSIRI, DALE C. GARELL, GEORGE HEAD,
MYLDRED E. JONES, MICHAEL PECK AND MEDICUS RENTZ

- ■ INTRODUCTION
- ■ THEORETICAL BACKGROUND
     AND RATIONALE
- ■ ETHICS
- ■ SELECTION AND TRAINING OF STAFF
- ■ RECORD KEEPING AND EVALUATION
- ■ RESOURCES AND REFERRALS
- ■ USE OF PROFESSIONAL CONSULTANTS

INTRODUCTION

THE IDEA FOR Hotline grew out of an awareness of the seemingly increasing alienation of youth in large metropolitan areas and the relative lack of effective avenues of communication during stress (including the traditional helping agencies). Since the inception of the service, additional factors have emerged which, if continued to be borne out by the data, should have significant implications for mental health concepts in general.

Perhaps the most unique and crucial features of the resources are its immediate availability and respect for the anonymity of the caller. The approach utilized is not one which presumes traditional professional training in psychotherapy or counseling on the part of those who answer the calls. Rather, it is based on the concept of "creative listening" and underpinned by a warm and human regard for others and a special awareness of and sensitivity to the world of young people.

The purpose of this Chapter is to provide guidelines to the organization and development of a service such as Hotline, to assist participating agencies in arriving at some consensus as to standards to be adhered to in the establishment and maintenance of a Hotline service. A successful Hotline service includes the following components: an Advisory Board or Board of Directors, depending upon whether the Hotline is a new organization or is administered by an existing institution, careful planning, professional consultants, feedback and consultation, and a training program.

To launch a new service advice should be sought from an existing service. Consultation will provide opportunity to examine some of the problems and may assist the group in deciding whether a new Hotline is needed or whether the needs could better be served by extension of an existing Hotline through a tie-in service. The approach, operating procedures, selection and training of staff, resources and reference materials are described in detail in the following pages.

THEORETICAL BACKGROUND AND RATIONALE

A focal aspect of the Hotline service is the approach followed in assisting the young people who call. This approach rests on a number of key assumptions related to the nature of crisis, to their resolution and to adolescence in general. There is nothing new here—simply the choice of one particular set of biases over others that might be followed in trying to assist young people as they grapple with difficult problems.

The crisis model adopted follows closely the precepts of General Systems Theory in a fashion similar to that of Caplan in his considerations of preventive psychiatry. Within this framework, a crisis is viewed as an upset or disequilibrium in an individual's efforts to organize experience such that it's reasonably predictable and need-fulfilling. A crisis is experienced when one is faced with a problematic situation which, for the moment at least, appears both insolvable and inescapable. Insolvable in the light of perceived limitations in coping resources; inescapable insofar as important needs are at stake. The usual situation is one in which needs conflict—the satisfaction of one precluding the satisfaction of the other.

Inevitably, crisis will be resolved in one way or another if only to eliminate the unpleasant accompaniments of being "off-balance": tension, anxiety, cognitive disorientation increase the longer a resolution is delayed. The manner in which a crisis is resolved is considered crucial for ongoing adjustment. It can represent a significant gain in adaptability—in mental health—by virtue of an enhancement of the individual's problem solving resources. In this case, the person emerges from the crisis a more effective human being than he was beforehand. He is prepared to face adaptively a wider range of experience and thereby allow himself the opportunity for further growth and enrichment.

On the other hand, the outcome of a crisis resolution could mean the addition of maladaptive coping styles, i.e. patterns of response which, in effect, represent a lessened capacity to deal with novel experiences and thus an increased vulnerability to breakdown in the future. This would be the case, for example, if one has chosen to avoid the problem or to manipulate reality in fantasy or to escape reality pressures through alienation or through the use of drugs.

Thus, the crisis represents a rather important fork in the road —moments of truth, as it were. On the one hand, an opportunity to move further along towards self-mastery and fulfillment; on the other, the chance of a significant setback that, at the very least, will require the retracing of steps. The issue, then, is two-fold: how to capitalize on the crisis experience recognizing its potential for growth; and, secondly, how to avoid *panicking* into a dead-end. These two components are clearly not independent. However, it would seem we most often overlook the opportunity implicit in the crisis while attending primarily to the preventive aspect. This is, perhaps, no more conspicuously evident than in the manner in which we customarily approach the "problem" of drug abuse.

Hotline is intent on exploring ways that enable at least as much as underlining ways that do not.

The forces brought to bear on the decision making processes determining the choice of strategy for crisis resolution include a variety of predispositions which the individual brings to the event. These include his background of coping experiences, his current ego strength, special meanings associated with the present problematic situation as derived from previous experience, and so on. An additional source of significant influence can be that which is forthcoming from the interaction of the individual with "significant others" in his psychosocial environment. In fact, it is assumed that as the crisis intensifies (i.e. continues without resolution) the crisis-bearer will be increasingly prone to turn to others for assistance. This is regarded as no less true of the adolescent than of an adult or young child. It is further assumed that to the extent the intervention (outside assistance) is well-timed—that is, geared to the individual's "reaching out"—optimal benefit is approached and effort minimized.

In setting up the Hotline service one of the primary considerations was that of providing the means whereby the need for the immediate availability of an outside assistant could be met. Such provision is considered particularly important for the adolescent because of the characteristic instability of forces—the rather delicate balance that prevails generally, let alone during crisis periods, that tends to force impulsive action. Underlying the notion that a Hotline was needed was, in part, the observation that the condition of immediate availability was not being met for many young people by the "significant others" within their own world not to mention the traditional caregiving agencies with waiting lists, eligibility mazes and limited hours.

In addition to "timing" there are other conditions assumed prerequisite to the opportunity for intervention, particiularly with the adolescent. There is the question of whether or not the individual will avail himself of the outside help even if the latter is available when needed. There seem to be any number of factors that could stop the process short. For example, certain pre-conceived notions as to how the outsider will interact once disclosures are made. Fears of rejection, of ridicule, of pre-judgment are mixed in with the images that a youngster may have of the "significant others" in his world and these kinds of expectations obviously interfere with his seeking their assistance.

One is reminded here of how important a role the business of imagery plays in the adolescent faced with the prospect of seeing a psychiatrist or psychologist. It is rare that adolescents greet this news with enthusiasm and it seems to have to do with the connotations that come to mind. To be sure, one doesn't have to be crazy to see a psychiatrist but this kind of objectivity may not come easily to the adolescent fighting his fears of insanity, a fairly typical preoccupation it would seem. This argument can be extended beyond the psychiatrist to the traditionally conceived caregiving agencies that most communities provide. The question again is how available, in effect, are these resources when their services are defined in terms of a specific problem as opposed to simply seeing people who are troubled by this or that. One suspects that many adolescents at least are "turned off" by the connotations of the label, even assuming they are somehow able to so pinpoint the problem that they are clear on what line to stand in. The most troublesome connotation of being labeled a problem, particularly for the adolescent who is struggling to prove to himself, let alone to others, that he shows promise of becoming an adult, is probably that which to him at least implies weakness, inadequacy, inferiority and the like. All of this amounts, in effect, to saying that the individual is incapable of being responsible for his own life and, thus, that it must be taken out of his hands. Hopefully this is not necessarily what happens once the helping process gets started. However, it appears to be a frequent expectation on the part of adolescents and as such to promote considerable resistance to "reaching out" at all.

Added, then, to the list of conditions essential if effective intervention can be possible is a kind of *"no strings"* message. Assistance is standing by when the need is felt to reach out and there are no strings attached to the assistant's participation in one's struggles and concerns. The assistant is here to listen, to hear one out and to *collaborate* in problem solving. Anonymity is respected so that doubts may be tested with immunity.

A final key assumption underlying Hotline's approach relates to what constitutes help once a person has reached out and made contact. If the conditions of timing and unconditional regard have been met, the major thrust of the helping relationship is that of mobilizing the individual's resources toward effective problem solving rather than rendering advice or in other ways taking over. If the crisis experience is to yield dividends in terms of growth, the individual must be afforded the opportunity of continued involvement in working through the problem. The task of the outside assistant then is not prescriptive but rather one of provoking inquiry; of setting up an atmosphere in which the individual is prompted to examine what he's experiencing, to reconsider his opinions about himself and his relationships and to become aware of alternative pathways in meeting the challenge he faces. The outcome of this kind of experience is two-fold: (1) *the individual's ego strength is enhanced because he discovers a capacity to be responsibly involved in matters of personal significance; and* (2) *emergent strategies or solutions are most likely to be implemented because they have meaningful anchorage in the individual's own perceptual world.* In short, the goal is to counter the tendency to rely on external agents of change and through the very process of interaction itself allow for an experience in self-direction. It is assumed that this kind of opportunity will have significance beyond the resolution of the immediate crisis.

The tasks of the outside assistant, as conceived above requires considerable discipline, skill and effort. To collaborate in the sense intended here implies understanding as fully as possible how the crisis-bearer views his situation. To gain this kind of understanding requires listening in the true sense: Being completely engrossed in what is being said without imposing value judgments, without comparing, without translating what is being said into the terms of one's own experience. Hotline's monthly training sessions are devoted in large part to "listening workshops"; a continual effort is necessary to overcome old patterns of not listening.

It is assumed that through the very act of clarifying the crisis (on the part of both the assistant and crisis-bearer) much of the "working through" is achieved. Coping strategies become apparent as one approaches a total understanding of the situation one has viewed as problematic. Such understanding obviously requires an atmosphere of honest self-disclosure and a mutuality of intent on the part of the parties involved that carries no vestige of prejudgment.

In review, then, the major provisions of the Hotline concept are as follows:

1. *Immediate availability* so that assistance is timed to the "reaching out";
2. *An open door policy* meant to serve people with problems rather than problems with people attached;
3. *The recognition of the need for help rests with the adolescent himself* rather than being the inspiration of others, the latter often fuel for resistance;
4. *Respect for the anonymity of the caller* so that he's free to test out doubts about himself with immunity as well as the trustworthiness of the listener; and
5. An approach *reinforcing notions of strength* in the individual rather than weakness or dependency, by mobilizing the caller's resources toward effective problem solving.

ETHICS

General Statement

All professional agencies operate from prescribed ethical standards which, for the most part, are interdisciplinary and have evolved from a body of material. In the case of Hotline, a new service, there is no specific body of material to draw from; therefore, it becomes necessary to establish ethical guidelines. In so doing we have drawn heavily upon other disciplines. For the purpose of this handbook, Ethics is discussed along two lines—the first being Ethics for the organization and the second being Ethics for the individual who works within that organization.

General Guidelines for the Organization: The Hotline service is provided out of a concern for people. This concern is expressed through creative listening on a nonjudgmental basis, to help the caller discover his own solutions and/or resources with which to solve his problem.

Because of the dissimilarity of services there is a place for diverse approach, provided that it is honest and holds the caller's best interest as the paramount issue; that an agency can take (or not take) a direct stand on a moral issue as they choose and there is a place for both without any prejudice toward the value of the service provided.

The primary purpose of Hotline is to serve the needs of the caller rather than the needs of the listener or organization (which means help must be offered with each caller's personal frame of reference and values in mind). Hotline accepts the caller where he is, in whatever situation he is found, and assumes that he is representing the truth as far as he, in his present situation, sees it.

The desire for anonymity preferred by the caller is carefully respected so that the desire for recognition is regulated by that caller. Service does not depend upon giving a name.

Confidentiality is self-evident and understood at every stage of the service unless the caller requests otherwise or crisis demands breaking of this rule. The interaction between the caller and the listener is a privileged communication the same as a psychologist, doctor or minister receives for his client. This, of course, does not negate the professional discussion of the problem bound in trust between client and caller.

Ethics for the Individual Listener: The ethics of the agency bind the listener, who is connected with the service. Each service should provide its own inclusive guidelines for its listeners.

It was generally agreed that there should be no follow-up outside the office except by assignment by the permanent staff or board of the service.

Keeping the confidence of the individual is paramount and it was agreed that material in one calling situation should not be compared with others over the phone. Honesty with the caller should prevail, indicating that records are being kept of the call but that this material is held in confidence within the service agency office.

SELECTION AND TRAINING OF STAFF

Selection and training of staff are continuing and interdependent processes. Selection continues during training; there should be a process to select out persons who, having become listeners, prove to be disturbed and/or who are trying to solve their own problems.

Criteria for Selection of Staff *—Effective "listeners" have the capacity to listen creatively, to develop rapport, are flexible, nonjudgmental and are motivated to help. The capacity to listen is based upon self-awareness and an understanding of self.

Listeners might include *Teenagers* (mature), accompanied by an adult in a supervisory capacity or a working relationship. Whatever criteria are used should be universal. The agency should not exclude anyone who meets the criteria.

Some *characteristics of a good "listener"* are: (1) *Nonpossessive* warmth and regard; ability to empathize without displacing needs. (2) Absence of judgmental, authoritarian or other defensive postures. (3) Authenticity as a person and acceptance of the other's capacity to be likewise.

Training—As noted above, the selection of listeners takes place during training; therefore, there should be provision in the training process for opportunities to develop self-awareness and understanding of self, and of his capacities in dealing with problems. Training should be geared to allow the listener to become aware of problem phone calls and be comfortable in seeking consultation for these.

Training should have, at least, the following elements:

An orientation session (s) for new listeners, allowing a minimum of six hours.

Ten hours of on-the-job training with actual calls handled in a supervised situation.

Professional, including other Hotlines, involvement in the training.

Planned role-playing in which the trainees play both parts— caller and listener.

Technical training regarding specific effects of drugs, terminology, crisis situations, back-up resources, information, etc.

Honesty in answers.

Ways to talk and to listen (techniques of reflecting, of evaluation of a crisis) .

Focusing on the needs behind the questions.

Listeners should give information instead of advice unless in a crisis situation.

---

*See Pages 143-144 for "Personality Traits . . . in the Suicide Prevention Volunteer."

Persons working in similar or allied fields should be included in the training sessions to inform the listeners of developments in the field.

Sessions on available resources and how to use these.

Opportunity for free exchange of ideas, questions, problems, hangups, etc., comments on performance and interstaff relationships.

The training process is primarily focused on the approaches and techniques of creative listening. Therefore, these will be discussed here rather than in a separate section.

Approaches and Techniques: Whatever the specifics of the approach, it should allow for free and open disclosure on the part of the caller. Among other things, this means that the "listener" should be alert to the possibility of confusing his own frame of reference (values, labels, modus operandi, etc.) with that of the caller's. This would apply regardless of age or specific problem.

If a person is to be effective in assisting another toward change, the former must provide an atmosphere in which the latter can feel free to disclose himself, i.e. expose his view of things (perceptual field).

The individual has the capacity to reorganize his view of things and behavioral modifications result therefrom. This implies that the "listener's" function is not to superimpose solution (advice, opinions, values, etc.) but rather to provoke self-examination such that a realignment would mean the emergence of pathways not previously a part of the perceptual schema.

Clarification of the problem (conflict) is an important function of the "listener." Some confrontation may be necessary here—gently but firmly and in manageable doses.

Offering "solutions": there is probably no one "best way" to solve a problem in most instances; the most meaningful and effective resolutions rest with the caller. It is then a part of the listener's function to provoke "discovery" on the caller's part by generating an atmosphere in which self-examination is possible.

Dependency: handling callers who repeatedly make use of the service.

1. When it appears that the caller is comfortably substituting the Service for himself, confrontation may be in order.

2. Collaboration among staff members toward the end of formulating a plan that can be followed with consistency in approaching individual repeaters.

3. Examining the possibility that the "listener" is encouraging the dependency (counter-transference).

Handling real crisis calls—In a "crisis" call in terms of imminent danger to self and/or others, some emergency interaction is in order as opposed to a tactic which rests heavily on the caller's resources (the latter probably cannot be mobilized sufficiently at this time). The staff takes more direct, aggressive and decisive action than would otherwise be the case. It's a question of "stopping the bleeding." Question here is how to develop skill in judging the status of the crisis.

Non-crisis calls—The large majority of calls are felt not to involve a crisis of the order described above. In these cases, the "treatment of choice" appears to involve the following:

1. Assumptions of Principles of Approach
    a. Phenomenologically based: i:e. people behave as a function of their perception of self and environment.
    b. It follows from (a) that the question of "how" (process) assumes more significance than the question of "what" (content).
2. Techniques would include the following:
    Clarification and Reflection
        e.g. "Do you mean that. . . . . ?"
             "It sounds to me that you're saying. . . . ."
             "I wonder if. . . . ."
             "Could it be that. . . . ."
             "I'm confused. On one hand you say . . . and now you're saying. . . . ."
    Focusing
        e.g. "I'm not sure that we've really gotten to what's bothering you."
             "We seem to be going around in circles. I wonder about these feelings of failure you mentioned earlier."
    Confirmation of feelings
        e.g. "You're feeling very lonely and depressed. You don't feel that anyone cares at all."
             "You've been calling repeatedly now every time it's the same game. . . . ."

RECORD KEEPING AND EVALUATION

Records are a significant part of an emergency telephone service. They are of value to the service in the following ways:

1. They indicate to what extent the service is being used.
2. They indicate the nature of problems (trends) being dealt with by the service.
3. They give direction in a training program for listeners concerning major problems to be dealt with.

4. Records provide information helpful to the service in seeking financial support.
5. Records serve as one means of evaluating the performance of the listener.
6. They are necessary on a long-term basis for future study and research.
7. They provide a picture of the development of the service.
8. Records are tangible evidence of what a listener is doing and can be used to promote morale.
9. A record form provides a guideline for the listener in evaluating the call as he deals with approriate areas.

It is recommended that all forms have the following basic information:*

Contact Number	Date
Time	Length of Call
Caller	Listener
Sex	Age
Marital Status	Occupation
Nature of Problem	Recommendations

Additional information appropriate for the type of service may be added. It would be ideal for similar services to have a standard form and for all services to collect the same basic information.

Each service should be advised of the legal status of their records. Proper precaution should be taken to protect the caller and the service. Records are privileged communication and should be handled with professional discretion.

RESOURCES AND REFERRALS

Resources

An important and necessary element of a Hotline Service is a resource file. This should be compiled as a first step in the organization of a Hotline. A Resource Library is a must! A good basic book is the *Directory of Health, Welfare, Vocational and Recreation Services in Los Angeles County.*

---

*See Appendix A for Sample Forms

Other resources which should be explored and added to the list are: Local groups, e.g. groups working with the drug problem, Free Clinics, legal clinics, clergy counseling services, crash pads (after they have been checked out), names of professional persons who have agreed to assist Hotline callers, etc. The resources may be as extensive as the local Hotline is able to develop. The important guideline, in this respect, is *know your resources, always check them out before you refer a caller.* Periodic checks should be made after the first contact. The resource library should include information on drugs, juvenile legislation, civil rights, draft legislation, on venereal disease, and emergency admission policies of local hospitals, etc.

Referrals

The nature of the problem determines the use and type of a referral. The Listener makes a referral only after he and the caller have fully explored the situation to be certain the basic problem has emerged. Listeners should become fully informed in specific areas of frequent calls, e.g. drugs, sex, family relationships, boy/girl relationships so as to negate the necessity for referrals and deal with the problem "here and now."

Some general principles governing referrals are: don't promise service by another agency; don't refer callers to an agency or professional person if they are already in treatment; if necessary, make the call to the other agency for the caller; when possible the listener should "patch" the call in to the referral resource; don't refer to a resource on speculation for service; encourage referred person to check back with the service; explore every resource and evaluate its effectiveness.

Finally, it should be mentioned that one of the positive off-shoots of Hotline is the development of new community resources to meet the needs of youth.

USE OF PROFESSIONAL CONSULTANTS

Professional specialists in fields relevant to youth (e.g. law, medicine, health, mental health, religion, recreation, education) should be available to Hotline as "on-call" consultants. His function is to assist the listener in the course of a difficult call; when indicated by the circumstances, the consultant and caller may be "patched-in" and talk with each other. The consultant should be one who is well versed in one or more of the above-mentioned fields; he should know the circumstances under which a minor may be referred for help without the parents' consent, such as: a 12-year-old with a communicable disease or a 14-year-old not living at home and parents not paying for support may be referred for medical care. If a consultant feels a referral is needed, existing agencies should be used whenever possible.

APPENDIX A

HOTLINE CONTACT WORK SHEET

CONFIDENTIAL   Time_____ (am) (pm)
                                          Duration of call_____
Night call__Day call__Day__Date_____   Consultant_____
Parent's Name_____ Marital: S M W D CL
Address_____   Phone #_____
Youngster involved_____ Sex: M F
Age____Birth Date_____Grade_____School_____
Which drug is being abused_____
How much_____How often_____
Any suicide attempts or bad trips_____
Statement of problem:
Prev. medical, psychological &/or psychiatric treatment:
Current medical, psychological &/or psychiatric treatment:
Family Doctor_____ Phone #_____
How know about HL_____ Prior HL Contact_____
                                   With Whom_____
Why calling now_____ For info____Help_____
Other siblings, E & ages_____
Interview date_____ With Whom_____
Parent's religion_____ Occupation_____
Employer_____Annual income_____
Current family situation:
Recommendations_____
_____
Referral:_____
Do you recommend Educational Classes?_____
CONTINUE COMMENTS ON REVERSE SIDE, INCLUDING
INFO ON FOLLOWUPS.

PCC WORK SHEETS

No. of PCC contacts__ Time_____ (am) (pm) Duration of call_____
Night call_____ Day call_____Day_____ Date_____
Patient_____Staff member_____
Address_____ Tel. No. _____
City_____ County_____
Who called (Name & relationship) _____

Address & City_____ Tel. No. _____

How know about PCC_____

Prior PCC contact_____With whom_____

Why referred: SA; ST; SB; SI; None   For info. __Consult__Action___

Age__Birth Date_____Sex: M   F   Marital: S M W D S MM

Race____Religion_____   Follow up

Occupation_____call made: Yes___No____

Education completed_____ Sex, no. & ages of children_____

_____

Statement of problem: Suicide potential (1–9)

Chronic_____ Acute_____ Prev. sui. behavior_____

Previous medical and/or psychiatric trtmt:

Current medical and/or psychiatric trtmt:

Disposition: (Include calls to relatives, friends, police, physician, recommendations to patient or caller, etc.):

Suicidal Potentiality Criteria: 1) Age and sex; 2) Prior suicidal behavior; 3) Method-threatened or attempted; 4) Loss of loved one; 5) Communication aspect; 6) Medical symptoms; 7) Resources; 8) Mood, feelings, behavior; 9) Diagnostic impression, referral, self or other; 10) Feelings of informant.

CONTINUE COMMENTS ON REVERSE SIDE, INCLUDING INFORMATION ON FOLLOW-UPS, PLEASE.

021/3

CHILDRENS HOSPITAL
HOTLINE CONTACT FORM   Code #_____

NAME:

I.D.: _____

SEX: Male__ Female__   Date: _____

AGE: _____   Time: _____

AREA: _____PHONE:_____   Length Call: _____

PROXY: _____   for:_____

                 subject_____

Called Before: proxy_____   Source: _____

  Yes___ No___   both_____

CLARIFICATION: (use back side if   AFFECT

                necessary)   PRE-   POST

                       _____ Depression   _____

                       _____ Elation   _____

                       _____ Flat   _____

                       _____ Panic   _____

```
_____ Hostility-Anger _____
_____ Worry           _____
_____ Normal          _____
_____ "High"          _____
_____ Other_____    _____
```

STRATEGIES:
  Tried:
  Emergent:
RESOLUTION:
  Referral: _____ CONSULTANT TIE-IN: __No
                                                   __Yes
  Self-Help (explain) :   With Whom: _____
EVALUATION: Level of Confidence
  _____ Very meaningful   _____1 Very certain
  _____ Probably helpful   _____2
  _____ Thought provoking   _____3
  _____ Lip service response   _____4
  _____ Waste of time   _____5
                               _____6 Very uncertain
_____Put-on
_____Curiosity   _____
                                        STAFF

APPLICATION
CHILDRENS HOSPITAL
HOTLINE EMERGENCY TELEPHONE SERVICE

Name_____Age_____
Address_____Phone No._____
_____

Married _____ # of Children_____ Language Spoken_____
Single _____
Divorced _____
Other   _____

Last grade completed_____ Major_____
Currently enrolled in_____

Employment: Current Employment (Occupation)_____
            Address_____ Phone No._____
            _____

Name of Employer_____

---

1. Describe any experiences and/or formal education you have which
   you feel would be relevant to the Hotline Phone Service:

   _____
   _____
   _____
   _____

2. Why do you want to participate in this program?

   _____
   _____
   _____
   _____

3. When would you be available? (Circle Day and Hours)
   Sun Mon. Tues. Wed. Thurs. Fri. Sat.   6 p.m.-12 midnight

   _____
                             Fri. Sat.   8 p.m.-2 a.m.

   _____   _____
         Signature   Date

TRAINEE EVALUATION SHEETS

Name Trainee:_____

Trainer:_____

1. Please rate your trainee on the following:

	A*	B*	C*	D*	E*	F*
A. Enthusiasm for program	—	—	—	—	—	—
B. Acceptance of student role	—	—	—	—	—	—
C. Grasp of basic principles	—	—	—	—	—	—
D. Communication skill on phone	—	—	—	—	—	—
E. Ease of inter-staff exchange	—	—	—	—	—	—
F. Capacity for original contributions	—	—	—	—	—	—

*A = Outstanding
 B = Excellent
 C = Good
 D = Fair
 E = Questionable
 F = No basis for evaluating

2. Briefly summarize your opinion of the trainee's major strengths re:
   working on Hotline.

3. What are the areas of relative weakness (if any), i.e. that you would concentrate on in further training?

Trainee:_____

4. Do you have any reservations about the trainee's continued participation in Hotline?

_____No

_____Yes   If Yes, please explain:

5. Have you felt comfortable in the teaching role?

_____Yes

_____No   If No, please explain:

6. Additional Comments:

_____

                                    Signed

Date:_____

POSITIVE PERSONALITY TRAITS OF VOLUNTEERS

1. Healthy interest in S.P.I. with a sincere desire to be of help to another individual
2. Intraception
2. Self-insight
4. Compassion, warmth, empathy
5. Attitudes of tolerance and acceptance
6. Objectivity
7. Punctuality
8. Dependability
9. Initiative
10. At least average I.Q. (There doesn't seem to be any particular advantage to the volunteer's having superior intelligence unless he is willing to use it.)
11. Physical health
12. Emotional stability
13. Emotional maturity
14. Endurance
15. Low anxiety
16. Tolerance for stress
17. Cheerfulness, sense of humor
18. Tolerance for frustration encountered in hang-up calls, rejec-

tion of offered referrals and help, and the frustration of never knowing what happens to our callers

19. A liking for order (Because we have no full-time secretary, the only way we can make it possible for all incoming shifts to find what they need quickly and easily is to have organization.)
20. Willingness to cooperate within the framework of established procedures and the supervisory system; "team spirit"
21. Willingness to learn; openness to new knowledge
22. Willingness to do more than serve a 4-hour shift
23. Respect for others (This would include respect for the privacy of our callers and our volunteers as well as respect for the S.P.I. organization as a whole)
24. Optimism
25. Flexibility

PERSONALITY TRAITS CONSIDERED DESIRABLE IN THE SUICIDE PREVENTION VOLUNTEER

1. A real desire to be of help to another individual (persons who have fantasies of being God or a hero are quickly disenchanted with SPI programs).
2. A sensitivity to the underlying motives of human behavior.
3. Compassion for other people.
4. Nonjudgmental attitudes.
5. Punctuality.
6. Dependability (factors such as having many young children who frequently make unexpected demands, having a spouse who objects to membership in SPI, ill health, etc. may interfere with dependability).
7. At least average intelligence (it doesn't seem to be any particular advantage to the volunteer having superior intelligence unless he is willing to use it).
8. Physical health.
9. Emotional stability.
10. Emotional maturity.
11. Endurance (the volunteer worker who is very impatient and unable to withstand stress because of a low stress tolerance, becomes overly excitable, thinks impulsively rather than logically, disregards procedures and methods used and becomes emo-

tionally involved with the person on the other end of the line).

12. Little anxiety.

13. Cheerfulness.

14. Liking for order (because we have no full-time secretary and because so many records are kept on everything we do, the disorganized volunteer renders a hardship on other people).

15. The willingness to cooperate within the framework of established procedures and the supervisory system.

16. A willingness to learn (this would include good attendance in training, meeting seminars as well as a willingness to keep up with new instructive materials).

17. A willingness to do more than serve just a four-hour shift.

18. A respect for others (this would include respect for the privacy of our callers and our volunteers as well as respect for the SPI organization as a whole).

19. A willingness, and cooperativeness in undergoing screening.

20. A healthy dab of optimism (the pessimist subjects an organization like this to a great deal of group destructive behavior).

21. Some insight into one's own personality and problems and a willingness to look at the relationship between personal problems one might have and how it might influence the behavior on the telephone.

22. Patience and the ability to take many long hours of boredom; this is needed for those shifts where there are few calls from suicidal people, or in fact any call of any kind, all shifts are like this at some time.

23. A tolerance for frustration—the frustration of calls which end in the middle, of calls which never come, or referrals which are accepted but never acted on, and the frustration of never knowing what happened to some calls, or learning that the agency involved was not able to cope.

NEGATIVE PERSONALITY TRAITS OF VOLUNTEERS

1. Unhealthy interest in SPI work
   A. Having the idea that SPI work involves dramatic, suspenseful rescues by hero-like volunteers
   B. Having the idea that there are certain cases which only

they can handle or understand

C. Dependency fostering

2. Lack of insight
3. Judgmental attitudes
4. Tardiness
5. Undependability (Failing to appear for duty without notifying anyone; failing to perform assigned tasks; failing to do what they promise that they will do. Having many young children who frequently make unexpected demands, having a spouse who objects to SPI membership, ill health, etc., may interfere with dependability.)
6. Less than average intelligence
7. Physical illness, recent hospitalization for physical or emotional sickness
8. Alcoholism
9. Having insatiable needs for attention or recognition
10. Depression
11. High anxiety and low tolerance for stress
12. Immaturity
13. Low endurance
14. Dislike for order
15. Unwillingness to cooperate with other volunteers and supervisors; unwillingness to follow procedures or to check with supervisors whenever they feel procedures would be forgotten
16. Inability to take criticism
17. Unwillingness to discuss such topics as homosexuality, sexuality, obscenity
18. Senility
19. Lack of self-control in sexual urges
20. Psychosis
21. Destructiveness (This refers to persons who are jealous and critical to the point that morale begins to be affected. Their aim seems to be to destroy, for they show no willingness to think of workable solutions to the problems they unearth.)
22. Anti-learning attitudes
23. Religiosity
24. Hyper-criticalness
25. Pessimism
26. Rigidity in thinking

THE UNDESIRABLE TRAITS IN VOLUNTEERS

1. Having the idea that suicide prevention volunteer work involves dramatic suspenseful rescues by hero-like volunteers.
2. Having the idea that there are certain types of cases (usually in which they are overly involved emotionally) which only they can handle or understand.
3. Lack of insight.
4. Judgmental attitude.
5. Tardiness.
6. Undependability (failure to appear for duty without notifying anyone, failure to perform assigned tasks, failure to do what they promise that they will do).
7. Less than average intelligence.
8. Physical illness. A too recent hospitalization for any major surgery or sickness, especially one of mental or emotional illness (in the first months of our operation, most of our workers who fit into this category dropped out of our program).
9. Alcoholism—or being addictive personality (our experience has been that anyone who is actively involved in Alcoholics Anonymous, who shows an interest in our program and comes into our program, drops out after a short period of time).
10. Having insatiable needs for attention and recognition.
11. Persons in depressions.
12. High anxiety level accompanied by a low tolerance for stress.
13. Immaturity (this cannot be measured by years; some of our best, most reliable workers are high school or college students).

SUGGESTED BIBLIOGRAPHY

1. Allport, G.: *Becoming.* New Haven, Yale University Press (PB).
2. Barbara, Dominick A.: *The Art of Listening,* Springfield, Thomas, 1966.
3. Bertalanffy, Ludwig: *General Systems Theory.* New York, George Braziller, 1968, Ch. 9 (espec.).
4. Buber, M.: *Between Man and Man.* Boston, Beacon Press, 1955 (PB).
5. Buber, M.: *I and Thou.* New York, Scribners, 1958. (PB).
6. Bugental, J.: *The Search for Authenticity: An existential-analytic approach to psychotherapy.* New York, 1966.
7. Caplan, G.: *Principles of Preventive Psychiatry.* New York, Basic Books, 1964.
8. Hesse, H.: *Siddhartha.* New York, New Directions (PB).

9. Joslyn, I.: *The Word of the Adolescent.*
10. Jourard, S.: *The Transparent Self.* Princeton, van Nostrand, 1964 (PB).
11. Jourard, S.: *Disclosing Man to Himself.* Princeton, van Nostrand, 1968.
12. Jung, C. G.: *The Undiscovered Self.* Boston, Little, 1957.
13. Kelley, G.: *The Psychology of Personal Constructs.* New York, Norton, 1955.
14. Progoff, I.: *Depth Psychology and Modern Man.* New York, Julian Press, 1959.
15. Progoff, I.: *The Symbolic and the Real.* New York, Julian Press, 1963.
16. Rogers, C. R.: *On Becoming a Person.* Boston, Houghton Mifflin, 1961.
17. Rogers, C. R.: Some observations on the organization of personality, *American Psychological, 2:* 358–368, 1957.
18. Simmons, J. L., and Winograd, B.: *It's Happening.* Santa Barbara, Marc-Laird, 1966 (PB).
19. Tillich, P.: *The Courage to Be.* New Haven, Yale University Press, 1952.

APPENDIX B

HALFWAY HOUSES AND GROUP HOMES
FOR TROUBLED CHILDREN

Alabama	Division of Juvenile Delinquency Services
	Department of Pensions and Security
	64 North Union Street
	Montgomery, Alabama 36104
Alaska	Division of Corrections
	Pouch H
	Juneau, Alaska 99801
Arizona	Arizona State Department of Corrections
	1601 West Jefferson
	Phoenix, Arizona 85007
Arkansas	Department of Social and Rehabilitation Services
	Juvenile Services Division
	4313 West Markham
	Little Rock, Arkansas 72203
California	Department of the Youth Authority
	714 "P" Street
	Sacramento, California 95814
Colorado	Division of Youth Services
	3900 South Carr Street
	Denver, Colorado 80202
Connecticut	Department of Children and Youth Services
	345 Main Street
	Hartford, Connecticut 06115
Delaware	Department of Health and Social Services
	Division of Juvenile Corrections
	Group Homes Program
	Box 2679—Union Street Station
	Wilmington, Delaware 19805
Florida	Division of Youth Services
	Bureau of Group Treatment
	1317 Winewood Boulevard
	P. O. Box 2705
	Tallahassee, Florida 32301
Georgia	Department of Human Resources Consultant
	Division of Community Services
	447 State Office Building
	Atlanta, Georgia 30334

Hawaii	Director of Social Services and Housing P. O. Box 339 Honolulu, Hawaii 96809
Idaho	Idaho Department of Environmental Protection and Health Youth Rehabilitation Division Statehouse Boise, Idaho 83707
Illinois	Juvenile Division Department of Corrections 400 Armory Building Springfield, Illinois 62706
Indiana	Indiana Youth Authority 804 State Office Building Indianapolis, Indiana
Iowa	Bureau of Family and Children's Services Department of Social Services Lucas Building Des Moines, Iowa 50317
Kansas	State Department of Social Welfare State Office Building Topeka, Kansas
Kentucky	Department of Child Welfare 403 Wapping Street Frankfort, Kentucky
Louisiana	Department of Corrections Division of Juvenile Service P. O. Box 85 Baker, Louisiana 70714
Maine	Department of Mental Health & Corrections State Office Building Bureau of Corrections Augusta, Maine 04330
Maryland	Department of Juvenile Services 6314 Windsor Mill Road Baltimore, Maryland 21207
Massachusetts	Department of Youth Services 73 Trenton Street Boston, Massachusetts
Michigan	Department of Social Services Office of Youth Services

	300 South Capitol Street Lansing, Michigan
Minnesota	Department of Corrections 310 State Office Building St. Paul, Minnesota 55155
Mississippi	Mississippi Training Schools 706 Robert E. Lee Building Jackson, Mississippi 39201
Missouri	State Board of Training Schools Box 447 Jefferson City, Missouri 65101
Montana	Department of Institutions 1236 East 6th Avenue Helena, Montana 59601
Nebraska	Department of Public Institutions P. O. Box 94728 Lincoln, Nebraska 68309
Nevada	Department of Health, Education and Welfare 308 North Curry Street Carson City, Nevada 89701
New Hampshire	New Hampshire Youth Development Center P. O. Box 303 Manchester, New Hampshire 03104
New Jersey	Department of Institutions and Agencies Division of Correction and Parole 135 West Hanover Street Trenton, New Jersey 08625
New Mexico	Group and Foster Home Program Juvenile Parole Services Department of Corrections Santa Fe, New Mexico 87301
New York	Division of Youth Executive Department 2 University Place Albany, New York 12203
North Carolina	Office of Youth Development 116 West Hargett Street P. O. Drawer 2687 Raleigh, North Carolina 27602
North Dakota	North Dakota Industrial School Box 548

	Mandan, North Dakota
	Department of Institutions
	Bismark, North Dakota
Ohio	Ohio Youth Commission
	4422 Hamilton Court North
	Columbus, Ohio 43227
Oklahoma	Department of Institutions
	Social and Rehabilitation Services
	Bureau of State Homes and Schools
	P. O. Box 25352
	Oklahoma City, Oklahoma 73112
Oregon	Office of the Director
	318 Public Service Building
	Children's Services Division
	516 Public Service Building
	Salem, Oregon 97310
Pennsylvania	Bureau of Youth Services
	Room 422, Health & Welfare Building
	Harrisburg, Pennsylvania 17120
Rhode Island	Department of Corrections
	75 Howard Avenue
	Cranston, Rhode Island 02920
	Whitmarsh House
	53 Whitmarsh Street
	Providence, Rhode Island 02907
South Carolina	South Carolina Department of Youth Services
	Youth Bureau Division
	4900 Shivers Street
	Columbia, South Carolina 29210
South Dakota	Board of Charities and Corrections
	Capitol Building
	Pierre, South Dakota 57301
Tennessee	Department of Corrections
	Division of Juvenile Probation
	1028 Andrew Jackson Building
	Nashville, Tennessee 37219
Texas	Texas Youth Council
	1005 Sam Houston Building
	Austin, Texas 78701

Utah   Utah State Industrial School
P. O. Box 41
Ogden, Utah

Vermont   Department of Corrections
State Office Building
Montpelier, Vermont 05602

Virginia   Division of Youth Services
429 South Belvidere Street
Richmond, Virginia 23220

Washington   Group Home Services
Department of Social and Health Services
P. O. Box 1788
Olympia, Washington

Washington, D.C. Social Rehabilitation Administration
Department of Human Resources
122 "C" Street, N.W.
Washington, D.C. 20001

West Virginia Division of Corrections
Capitol Complex
Charleston, West Virginia 25305

Wisconsin   Wisconsin Division of Corrections
Department of Health & Social Services
Box 669
Madison, Wisconsin

Wyoming   Board of Charities and Reform
Room 216 Capitol Building
Cheyenne, Wyoming 82001

Alberta, Canada House and Institutions Branch
Department of Health & Social Development
Administration Building
109th Street & 98th Avenue
Edmonton, Alberta, Canada

British Columbia Director of Corrections
1075 Melville Street
Vancouver 5, British Columbia
Canada

Manitoba   Provincial Probation Services
Department of Health & Social Development
Box 9-139 Tuxedo Avenue
Winnipeg, Manitoba, Canada

New Brunswick	Department of Justice
	Correctional Services Division
	County Court House
	Fredericton, New Brunswick
	Canada
Nova Scotia	Department of Public Welfare
	P.O. Box 696
	Halifax, Nova Scotia
	Canada
Ontario	Ministry of Correctional Services
	Parliament Buildings
	Toronto, Ontario, Canada
Yukon Territory	Department of Health, Welfare and Rehabilitation
	Box 2703
	Whitehorse, Yukon, Canada

APPENDIX C

PROGRAMS FOR RUNAWAY YOUTH

ALASKA
Alaska Childrens Service, 4600 Abbott Road, Anchorage, Alaska 99502
Open Door Clinic, 112 West 5th Street, Anchorage, Alaska 99502

ARIZONA
Hatful of Peas, 2501 BE. Camelback, Phoenix, Arizona 85106

CALIFORNIA
Berkeley Youth Alternatives, 2430 Dana St., Berkeley, Calif.
The Bridge, 2525 'A' St., San Diego, California 92102
Diogenes House, 418 2nd Avenue, Davis, California 95616
Emergency Shelter Program, 24679 2nd St., Hayward, Calif.
Huckleberry House, 3830 Judah St., San Francisco, Calif. 94122
Lodi House, 107 W. Lockefors St., Lodi, Calif. 95240
Manteca Awareness House, 603 East Yosemite, Manteca, Calif. 95336
Project Oz, 3304 Idlewild Way, San Diego, Calif.
Stockton House, 701 W. Branchi, Stockton, Calif.

COLORADO
Comitis, 1150 South Chambers Rd., P.O. Box 31552, Aurora, Colo. 80010
Haven House, 1313 Pine, Boulder, Colorado 80302
Order of the Holy Family, 2015 Glenarm Place, Denver, Colo. 80205
La Casa Contenta, 14 West Costilla Ave., Colorado Springs, Colo. 80902

CONNECTICUT
Project #9, 266 State Street, New Haven, Conn.

DISTRICT of COLUMBIA
Washington Runaway House, 1743 18th St., N.W., Washington, DC 20009
The Saja Collective, 1830 Connecticut Avenue, N.W., Washington, DC 20009

GEORGIA	The Bridge, 65 — 11th St. N.E., Atlanta, Georgia 30309
	The Salvation Army Girls Lodge, 848 Peachtree St. N.E., Atlanta, Ga. 30309
	Truck Stop Boys Lodge, 951 Piedmont Ave. NE., Atlanta, Ga. 30309
ILLINOIS	Looking Glass for Runaways, 1725 W. Wilson Ave., Chicago, Ill.
	Youth Help Center, 555 W. Belden Ave., Chicago, Illinois 60614
INDIANA	The Center, 3525 Jefferson St., Gary, Indiana 46408
	Stopover, 1537 North Central, Indianapolis, Indiana 46202
LOUISIANA	The Greenhouse Runaway Center, 3020 Magazine Street, New Orleans, Louisiana
MARYLAND	Fellowship of the Lights, 222 West Monument Street, Baltimore, Maryland 21201
	Second Mile House, c/o First United Methodist Church, Queen's Chapel and Queensbury Rd., Hyattsville, Md. 20782
MASSACHUSETTS	Boston Children's Service, 1 Walnut Street, Boston, Mass. 02108
	Bridge over Troubled Waters, 3 Walnut St., Boston, Mass. 02108
	Help, 498 Tremont St., Boston, Mass. 02116
	Our House, c/o Room to Move, Student Union, University of Massachusetts, Amherst, Mass. 01002
	Project Place, 31½ Dwight St., Boston, Mass. 02118
MICHIGAN	Autos House, 729 West South St., Kalamazoo, Mich. 49005
	The Bridge, 455 Morris Ave., Grand Rapids, Mich.
	Detroit Transit Alternative, 13100 Averhill Court, Detroit, Mich.

Ozone House, 502 E. Washington Street, Ann Arbor, Mich. 48108

The Port, Grand Blanc, Mich.

MINNESOTA   The Bridge for Runaway Youth, Inc., 608-20 Avenue S. Minneapolis, Minn.

Our House, P.O. Box 214, Red Wing, Minn. 55066

MISSOURI   Youth Emergency Service, 6808 Washington Ave., St. Louis, MO

NEBRASKA   Mid-City Crash, 3115 Cass Street, Omaha, Nebraska 68106

Omaha Awareness and Action, Omaha, Nebraska

NEVADA   Focus, 1601 East Sahara Ave., Las Vegas, NV 89105

NEW YORK   Project Yes, 48½ East 7th St., New York, NY

Refer Switchboard, 332 Hudson Ave., Albany, NY

NORTH CAROLINA   Youth Services Bureau, P.O. Box 3428, Greensboro, NC

OHIO   Free, 8911 W. Ridgewood Dr., Parma, Ohio 44130

The Haven, 32599 Cedar Rd., Lyndhurst, Ohio 44124

Head Help, 8254 Mayfield, Chesterland, Ohio

Huckleberry House, 1869 Summit St., Columbus, OH 43210

Rabbit, 3760 Dover Central Rd., Westlake, OH

Talbert House, 2316 Auberncrest, Cincinnati, OH 45219

The Tent, 15837 Euclid Ave., East Cleveland, OH

OREGON   Contact Center, 633 S.W. Montgomery, Portland, Oregon 97201

Looking Glass, 1960 Willamette, Eugene, Oregon

Sunflower House, 128 S.W. 9th, Corvallis, Oregon

PENNSYLVANIA

Deane House, 6000 Wayne Ave., Philadelphia, PA
Karma House, 262 S. Bouquet St., Pittsburgh, PA 15213
Voyage House, 2041 Walnut St., Philadelphia, PA
Youth Service Center, 133 West High Street, Carlisle, PA 17013

TEXAS

The Bridge, 1727 Winnie St., Galvaston, Texas
Bridge Association, Inc., 1417 8th Ave., Fort Worth, TX
The Family Connection, 2014 Commonwealth, Houston, TX

UTAH

Listening Post, Halladay, Utah

VERMONT

SHAC, 81 Maple, Burlington, Vermont 05401

WASHINGTON

Heads Up, 1910½ 104 'M' St., Bellevue, Washington
Renton Area Youth Service, 1525 North 4th St. Renton, WA 98055
Youth Advocates Inc., 1310 East Pike, Seattle, WA

WISCONSIN

Briar Patch, 2202 N. Bassett, Madison, Wisconsin
Pathfinders For Runaways, LTD., 924 E. Ogden Avenue, Milwaukee, Wisconsin 53202

BRITISH COLUMBIA

Cool-Aid Services, P.O. Box 33926, Station D, Vancouver, B.C.

INDEX

163